Victoria
Evidence Act Handbook
with
Common Objections
&
Evidentiary Foundations

Professor John Barkai

Cover colors are from the Victoria flag

Victoria Evidence Act Handbook
with Common Objections
&
Evidentiary Foundations

Victoria Evidence Act was last amended in 2020

In addition to just the Evidence Act, this handbook offers practical guidance and advice on how to make objections and establish evidentiary foundations. Such information is especially important for junior lawyers, less experienced or less confident lawyers, or anyone who may want a refresher or some new ideas about introducing evidence in court, especially digital evidence such as emails, text, and social media evidence.

Disclaimer: This book offers no legal advice, but does contain ideas about evidence worth sharing. In addition to the evidence act materials, this handbook contains substantial information about making objections, laying foundations to introduce evidence at trial, and methods to impeach witnesses. The appendix should be useful to lawyers and judges. Please build on those ideas if you find them useful, modify them for your own purposes, or reject them if you think they are inappropriate. In addition to traditional evidence issues, for the past 20 to 30 years lawyers and judges around the world have been struggling with the use of digital evidence in courts because evidence rules were drafted decades ago assuming that courts would only use paper documents. However, today the many forms of digital evidence, such as emails, text messages, social media sites, and other types of communication, dominant modern communication. Examples in the appendix of how to introduce traditional and digital evidence are based upon the U.S. Federal Rules of Evidence which are more designed for jury trials, but also know that the appendix examples are designed for non-jury trials.

Hopefully the ideas in this handbook will assist you to improve your practice.

Regarding copyright – there is none.

Font – Times New Roman 10

Corrections, omissions, suggestions? Contact barkai@hawaii.edu

Victoria Evidence Act Handbook
with
Common Objections
&
Evidentiary Foundations

Professor John Barkai
William S. Richardson School of Law
University of Hawaii
Honolulu, HI 96822
June 2023

ISBN: 9798392455621

Introduction
This Victoria Evidence Act Handbook contains:
the Victoria Evidence Act and a substantial appendix including:

A) **Making and Responding to Common Objections** (16 pages)
    - a discussion of the 16 common objections
    - a list of 60 common objections

B) **Evidentiary Foundations and Impeachment** (over 60 pages)
    - 25 examples of common evidentiary foundations
    - a brief discussion of differing standards for authenticating digital evidence such as email, text messages, social media sites, internet sites.

The appendix materials are based upon United States' Federal Rules of Evidence and offer some citations to those rules. I do not suggest that those U.S. rules apply in your country, but I believe the appendix material can be helpful when working with your evidence issues. These materials are offered with the benign intent to help you shape your legal practice

John Barkai

Summary of Contents

Appendix

Expanded Appendix Index

Making and Responding to Common Objections A-1

Evidentiary Foundations..A-17

Division 1A—Professional confidential relationship privilege
Division 1B—Sexual assault communications privilege
Division 1C—Journalist privilege
Division 2—Other privileges
Division 3—Evidence excluded in the public interest
Division 4—General
Part 3.11—Discretionary and mandatory exclusions
Chapter 4—Proof
Part 4.1—Standard of proof
Part 4.2—Judicial notice
Part 4.3—Facilitation of proof.
Division 1—General
Division 2—Matters of official record

Chapter 1—Preliminary

Introductory Note

Outline of this Act

This Act sets out the State rules of evidence. Generally speaking, the Act applies to proceedings in State courts and before other persons or bodies required to apply the laws of evidence (see section 4).

Chapter 2 is about how evidence is adduced in proceedings.

Chapter 3 is about admissibility of evidence in proceedings.

Chapter 4 is about proof of matters in proceedings.

Chapter 5 deals with miscellaneous matters.

The Dictionary at the end of this Act defines terms and expressions used in this Act.

Related legislation

This Act is in most respects uniform with the Evidence Act 1995 of the Commonwealth (the Commonwealth Act) and the Evidence Act 1995 of New South Wales (the New South Wales Act). The Acts are drafted in identical terms except so far as differences are identified by appropriate annotations to the texts, and except so far as minor drafting variations are required to accord with the drafting style of each jurisdiction.

If one Act contains a provision that is not included in another Act, there is a gap in the numbering of the other Act in order to maintain consistent numbering for the other provisions.

The Evidence Act 2001 of Tasmania also largely mirrors this legislation, but there are some departures.

Part 1.1—Formal matters

1. Purpose

The purpose of this Act is to make fresh provision for the law of evidence that is uniform with Commonwealth and New South Wales law.

2. Commencement

(1) This Part and the Dictionary at the end of this Act come into operation on the day after the day on which this Act receives the Royal Assent.

(2) Subject to subsection (3), the remaining provisions of this Act come into operation on a day or days to be proclaimed.

(3) If a provision of this Act does not come into operation before 1 January 2010, it comes into operation on that day.

3. Definitions

(1) Expressions used in this Act (or in a particular provision of this Act) that are defined in the Dictionary at the end of this Act have the meanings given to them in the Dictionary.

(2) The Dictionary at the end of this Act forms part of this Act.

Notes – 1. Some expressions used in this Act are defined in the Interpretation of Legislation Act 1984 and have the meanings given to them in that Act....

2. Subsection (2) differs from the Commonwealth Act and New South Wales Act.

3. The Commonwealth Act and New South Wales Act include an additional subsection regarding definitions which are unnecessary in Victoria due to the Interpretation of Legislation Act 1984.

3A. Notes

Notes do not form part of this Act.

Part 1.2—Application of this Act

4. Courts and proceedings to which Act applies

(1) This Act applies to all proceedings in a Victorian court, including proceedings that—

  (a) relate to bail; or

  (b) are interlocutory proceedings or proceedings of a similar kind; or

  (c) are heard in chambers; or

  (d) subject to subsection (2), relate to sentencing.

(2) If such a proceeding relates to sentencing—

  (a) this Act applies only if the court directs that the law of evidence applies in the proceeding; and

  (b) if the court specifies in the direction that the law of evidence applies only in relation to specified matters—the direction has effect accordingly.

(3) The court must make a direction if—

  (a) a party to the proceeding applies for such a direction in relation to the proof of a fact; and

  (b) in the court's opinion, the proceeding involves proof of that fact, and that fact is or will be significant in determining a sentence to be imposed in the proceeding.

(4) The court must make a direction if the court considers it appropriate to make such a direction in the interests of justice.

(5) In this section, a proceeding that relates to sentencing includes a proceeding for an order under Part 4 of the Sentencing Act 1991.

5. Extended application of certain provisions
*****

6. Territories
*****

7. Act binds Crown

This Act binds the Crown in right of Victoria and, in so far as the legislative power of Parliament permits, the Crown in all its other capacities.

8. Operation of Acts

This Act does not affect the operation of the provisions of any other Act.

9. Application of common law and equity

(1) This Act does not affect the operation of a principle or rule of common law or equity in relation to evidence in a proceeding to which this Act applies, except so far as this Act provides otherwise expressly or by necessary intendment.

(2) Without limiting subsection (1), this Act does not affect the operation of such a principle or rule so far as it relates to any of the following—

  (a) admission or use of evidence of reasons for a decision of a member of a jury, or of the deliberations of a member of a jury in relation to such a decision, in a proceeding by way of appeal from a judgment, decree, order or sentence of a court;

  (b) the operation of a legal or evidential presumption that is not inconsistent with this Act;

  (c) a court's power to dispense with the operation of a rule of evidence or procedure in an interlocutory proceeding.

10. Parliamentary privilege preserved
(1) This Act does not affect the law relating to the privileges of any Australian Parliament or any House of any Australian Parliament.
(2) In particular, section 15(2) does not affect, and is in addition to, the law relating to such privileges.

11. General powers of a court
(1) The power of a court to control the conduct of a proceeding is not affected by this Act, except so far as this Act provides otherwise expressly or by necessary intendment.
(2) In particular, the powers of a court with respect to abuse of process in a proceeding are not affected.

Chapter 2—Adducing evidence
Note
   Outline of this Chapter
This Chapter is about ways in which evidence is adduced.
Part 2.1 is about adducing evidence from witnesses.
Part 2.2 is about adducing documentary evidence.
Part 2.3 is about adducing other forms of evidence.

Part 2.1—Witnesses
Division 1—Competence and compellability of witnesses

12. Competence and compellability
Except as otherwise provided by this Act—
   (a) every person is competent to give evidence; and
   (b) a person who is competent to give evidence about a fact is compellable to give that evidence.

13. Competence—lack of capacity
(1) A person is not competent to give evidence about a fact if, for any reason (including a mental, intellectual or physical disability)—
   (a) the person does not have the capacity to understand a question about the fact; or
   (b) the person does not have the capacity to give an answer that can be understood to a question about the fact—
and that incapacity cannot be overcome.
   Note-See sections 30 and 31 for examples of assistance that may be provided to enable witnesses to overcome disabilities.
(2) A person who, because of subsection (1), is not competent to give evidence about a fact may be competent to give evidence about other facts.
(3) A person who is competent to give evidence about a fact is not competent to give sworn or affirmed evidence about the fact if the person does not have the capacity to understand that, in giving evidence, he or she is under an obligation to give truthful evidence

(4) A person who is not competent to give sworn or affirmed evidence about a fact may, subject to subsection (5), be competent to give unsworn evidence or evidence that is not affirmed about the fact.

(5) A person who, because of subsection (3), is not competent to give sworn or affirmed evidence is competent to give unsworn evidence or evidence that is not affirmed if the court has told the person—

    (a) that it is important to tell the truth; and

    (b) that he or she may be asked questions that he or she does not know, or cannot remember, the answer to, and that he or she should tell the court if this occurs; and

    (c) that he or she may be asked questions that suggest certain statements are true or untrue and that he or she should agree with the statements that he or she believes are true and should feel no pressure to agree with statements that he or she believes are untrue.

(6) It is presumed, unless the contrary is proved, that a person is not incompetent because of this section.

(7) Evidence that has been given by a witness does not become inadmissible merely because, before the witness finishes giving evidence, he or she dies or ceases to be competent to give evidence.

(8) For the purpose of determining a question arising under this section, the court may inform itself as it thinks fit, including by obtaining information from a person who has relevant specialised knowledge based on the person's training, study or experience.

14. Compellability—reduced capacity

A person is not compellable to give evidence on a particular matter if the court is satisfied that—

    (a) substantial cost or delay would be incurred in ensuring that the person would have the capacity to understand a question about the matter or to give an answer that can be understood to a question about the matter; and

    (b) adequate evidence on that matter has been given, or will be able to be given, from one or more other persons or sources.

15. Compellability—Sovereign and others

(1) None of the following is compellable to give evidence—

    (a) the Sovereign;

    (b) the Governor-General;

    (c) the Governor of a State;

    (d) the Administrator of a Territory;

    (e) a foreign sovereign or the Head of State of a foreign country.

(2) A member of a House of an Australian Parliament is not compellable to give evidence if the member would, if compelled to give evidence, be prevented from attending—

    (a) a sitting of that House, or a joint sitting of that Parliament; or

    (b) a meeting of a committee of that House or that Parliament, being a committee of which he or she is a member.

16. Competence and compellability—judges and jurors
(1) A person who is a judge or juror in a proceeding is not competent to give evidence in that proceeding. However, a juror is competent to give evidence in the proceeding about matters affecting the conduct of the proceeding.

(2) A person who is or was a judge in an Australian or overseas proceeding is not compellable to give evidence about that proceeding unless the court gives leave.

17. Competence and compellability—accused in criminal proceedings
(1) This section applies only in a criminal proceeding.

(2) An accused is not competent to give evidence as a witness for the prosecution.

(3) An associated accused is not compellable to give evidence for or against an accused in a criminal proceeding, unless the associated accused is being tried separately from the accused.

(4) If a witness is an associated accused who is being tried jointly with the accused in the proceeding, the court is to satisfy itself (if there is a jury, in the jury's absence) that the witness is aware of the effect of subsection (3).

18. Compellability of spouses and others in criminal proceedings generally
(1) This section applies only in a criminal proceeding.

(2) A person who, when required to give evidence, is the spouse, de facto partner, parent or child of an accused may object to being required—

    (a) to give evidence; or

    (b) to give evidence of a communication between the person and the accused—

as a witness for the prosecution.

(3) The objection is to be made before the person gives the evidence or as soon as practicable after the person becomes aware of the right so to object, whichever is the later.

(4) If it appears to the court that a person may have a right to make an objection under this section, the court is to satisfy itself that the person is aware of the effect of this section as it may apply to the person.

(5) If there is a jury, the court is to hear and determine any objection under this section in the absence of the jury.

(6) A person who makes an objection under this section to giving evidence or giving evidence of a communication must not be required to give the evidence if the court finds that—

    (a) there is a likelihood that harm would or might be caused (whether directly or indirectly) to the person, or to the relationship between the person and the accused, if the person gives the evidence; and

    (b) the nature and extent of that harm outweighs the desirability of having the evidence given.

(7) Without limiting the matters that may be taken into account by the court for the purposes of subsection (6), it must take into account the following—

    (a) the nature and gravity of the offence for which the accused is being prosecuted;

(b) the substance and importance of any evidence that the person might give and the weight that is likely to be attached to it;

(c) whether any other evidence concerning the matters to which the evidence of the person would relate is reasonably available to the prosecutor;

(d) the nature of the relationship between the accused and the person;

(e) whether, in giving the evidence, the person would have to disclose matter that was received by the person in confidence from the accused.

(8) If an objection under this section has been determined, the prosecutor may not comment on—

(a) the objection; or

(b) the decision of the court in relation to the objection; or

(c) the failure of the person to give evidence.

19. Compellability of spouses and others in certain criminal proceedings
*****

20. Comment on failure to give evidence *****

Division 2—Oaths and affirmations

21. Sworn evidence of witnesses to be on oath or affirmation

(1) A witness in a proceeding must either take an oath, or make an affirmation, before giving evidence.

(2) Subsection (1) does not apply to a person who gives unsworn evidence under section 13.

(3) A person who is called merely to produce a document or thing to the court need not take an oath or make an affirmation before doing so.

(4) The witness is to take the oath, or make the affirmation, in accordance with the appropriate form in Schedule 1 or in a similar form.

(5) Such an affirmation has the same effect for all purposes as an oath.

(6) For the purposes of subsection (4), in the case of a child or a person with a cognitive disability, the following words are taken to be a similar form of oath or affirmation—

"I promise to tell the truth.".

22. Interpreters to act on oath or affirmation

(1) A person must either take an oath, or make an affirmation, before acting as an interpreter in a proceeding.

(1A) An oath taken, or an affirmation made, by a person before acting as an interpreter on a day is taken for the purposes of subsection (1) to be an oath taken or affirmation made by that person for the purposes of any subsequent proceedings in that court on that day in which the person acts as an interpreter.

(2) The person is to take the oath, or make the affirmation, in accordance with the appropriate form in Schedule 1 or in a similar form.

(3) Such an affirmation has the same effect for all purposes as an oath.

23. Choice of oath or affirmation

(1) A person who is to be a witness or act as an interpreter in a proceeding may choose whether to take an oath or make an affirmation.

(2) The court is to inform the person that he or she has this choice, unless the court is satisfied that the person has already been informed or knows that he or she has the choice.

(3) The court may direct a person who is to be a witness to make an affirmation if—

(a) the person refuses to choose whether to take an oath or make an affirmation; or

(b) it is not reasonably practicable for the person to take an appropriate oath.

24. Requirements for oaths

(1) It is not necessary that a religious text be used in taking an oath.

(2) An oath is effective for the purposes of this Division even if the person who took it—

(a) did not have a religious belief or did not have a religious belief of a particular kind; or

(b) did not understand the nature and consequences of the oath.

24A. Alternative oath

(1) A person may take an oath even if the person's religious or spiritual beliefs do not include a belief in the existence of a god.

(2) Despite anything to the contrary in this Act, the form of oath taken by a person—

(a) need not include a reference to a god; and

(b) may instead refer to the basis of the person's beliefs in accordance with a form prescribed by the regulations.

25. Rights to make unsworn statements unaffected *****

Division 3—General rules about giving evidence

26. Court's control over questioning of witness

The court may make such orders as it considers just in relation to—

(a) the way in which witnesses are to be questioned; and

(b) the production and use of documents and things in connection with the questioning of witnesses; and

(c) the order in which parties may question a witness; and

(d) the presence and behaviour of any person in connection with the questioning of witnesses.

27. Parties may question witnesses

A party may question any witness, except as provided by this Act.

28. Order of examination in chief, cross-examination and re examination
Unless the court otherwise directs—
(a) cross-examination of a witness is not to take place before the examination in chief of the witness; and
(b) re-examination of a witness is not to take place before all other parties who wish to do so have cross-examined the witness.

29. Manner and form of questioning witnesses and their responses
(1) A party may question a witness in any way the party thinks fit, except as provided by this Chapter or as directed by the court.
(2) A court may, on its own motion or on the application of the party that called the witness, direct that the witness give evidence wholly or partly in narrative form.
(3) Such a direction may include directions about the way in which evidence is to be given in that form.
(4) Evidence may be given in the form of charts, summaries or other explanatory material if it appears to the court that the material would be likely to aid its comprehension of other evidence that has been given or is to be given.

30. Interpreters
A witness may give evidence about a fact through an interpreter unless the witness can understand and speak the English language sufficiently to enable the witness to understand, and to make an adequate reply to, questions that may be put about the fact.

31. Deaf and mute witnesses
(1) A witness who cannot hear adequately may be questioned in any appropriate way.
(2) A witness who cannot speak adequately may give evidence by any appropriate means.
(3) The court may give directions concerning either or both of the following—
(a) the way in which a witness may be questioned under subsection (1);
(b) the means by which a witness may give evidence under subsection (2).
(4) This section does not affect the right of a witness to whom this section applies to give evidence about a fact through an interpreter under section 30.

32. Attempts to revive memory in court

(1) A witness must not, in the course of giving evidence, use a document to try to revive his or her memory about a fact or opinion unless the court gives leave.

(2) Without limiting the matters that the court may take into account in deciding whether to give leave, it is to take into account—

    (a) whether the witness will be able to recall the fact or opinion adequately without using the document; and

    (b) whether so much of the document as the witness proposes to use is, or is a copy of, a document that—

        (i) was written or made by the witness when the events recorded in it were fresh in his or her memory; or

        (ii) was, at such a time, found by the witness to be accurate.

(3) If a witness has, while giving evidence, used a document to try to revive his or her memory about a fact or opinion, the witness may, with the leave of the court, read aloud, as part of his or her evidence, so much of the document as relates to that fact or opinion.

(4) The court is, on the request of a party, to give such directions as the court thinks fit to ensure that so much of the document as relates to the proceeding is produced to that party.

33. Evidence given by police officers

(1) Despite section 32, in any criminal proceeding, a police officer may give evidence in chief for the prosecution by reading or being led through a written statement previously made by the police officer.

(2) Evidence may not be so given unless—

    (a) the statement was made by the police officer at the time of or soon after the occurrence of the events to which it refers; and

    (b) the police officer signed the statement when it was made; and

    (c) a copy of the statement had been given to the person charged or to the person's Australian legal practitioner a reasonable time before the hearing of the evidence for the prosecution.

(3) A reference in this section to a police officer includes a reference to a person who, at the time the statement concerned was made, was a police officer.

34. Attempts to revive memory out of court

(1) The court may, on the request of a party, give such directions as are appropriate to ensure that specified documents and things used by a witness otherwise than while giving evidence to try to revive his or her memory are produced to the party for the purposes of the proceeding.

(2) The court may refuse to admit the evidence given by the witness so far as it concerns a fact as to which the witness so tried to revive his or her memory if, without reasonable excuse, the directions have not been complied with.

35. Effect of calling for production of documents

(1) A party is not to be required to tender a document only because the party, whether under this Act or otherwise—

    (a) called for the document to be produced to the party; or

    (b) inspected it when it was so produced.

(2) The party who produces a document so called for is not entitled to tender it only because the party to whom it was produced, or who inspected it, fails to tender it.

36. Person may be examined without subpoena or other process

(1) The court may order a person who—

    (a) is present at the hearing of a proceeding; and

    (b) is compellable to give evidence in the proceeding—

to give evidence and to produce documents or things even if a subpoena or other process requiring the person to attend for that purpose has not been duly served on the person.

(2) A person so ordered to give evidence or to produce documents or things is subject to the same penalties and liabilities as if the person had been duly served with such a subpoena or other process.

(3) A party who inspects a document or thing produced to the court because of subsection (1) need not use the document in evidence.

Division 4—Examination in chief and re examination

37. Leading questions

(1) A leading question must not be put to a witness in examination in chief or in re-examination unless—

    (a) the court gives leave; or

    (b) the question relates to a matter introductory to the witness's evidence; or

    (c) no objection is made to the question and (leaving aside the party conducting the examination in chief or re-examination) each other party to the proceeding is represented by an Australian legal practitioner or prosecutor; or

    (d) the question relates to a matter that is not in dispute; or

    (e) if the witness has specialised knowledge based on the witness's training, study or experience—the question is asked for the purpose of obtaining the witness's opinion about a hypothetical statement of facts, being facts in respect of which evidence has been, or is intended to be, given.

(2) Unless the court otherwise directs, subsection (1) does not apply in civil proceedings to a question that relates to an investigation, inspection or report that the witness made in the course of carrying out public or official duties.

(3) Subsection (1) does not prevent a court from exercising power under rules of court to allow a written statement or report to be tendered or treated as evidence in chief of its maker.

38. Unfavourable witnesses

(1) A party who called a witness may, with the leave of the court, question the witness, as though the party were cross-examining the witness, about—

    (a) evidence given by the witness that is unfavourable to the party; or

    (b) a matter of which the witness may reasonably be supposed to have knowledge and about which it appears to the court the witness is not, in examination in chief, making a genuine attempt to give evidence; or

    (c) whether the witness has, at any time, made a prior inconsistent statement.

(2) Questioning a witness under this section is taken to be cross-examination for the purposes of this Act (other than section 39).

(3) The party questioning the witness under this section may, with the leave of the court, question the witness about matters relevant only to the witness's credibility.

    Note-The rules about admissibility of evidence relevant only to credibility are set out in Part 3.7.

(4) Questioning under this section is to take place before the other parties cross-examine the witness, unless the court otherwise directs.

(5) If the court so directs, the order in which the parties question the witness is to be as the court directs.

(6) Without limiting the matters that the court may take into account in determining whether to give leave or a direction under this section, it is to take into account—

    (a) whether the party gave notice at the earliest opportunity of the party's intention to seek leave; and

    (b) the matters on which, and the extent to which, the witness has been, or is likely to be, questioned by another party.

(7) A party is subject to the same liability to be cross-examined under this section as any other witness if—

    (a) a proceeding is being conducted in the name of the party by or on behalf of an insurer or other person; and

    (b) the party is a witness in the proceeding.

39. Limits on re-examination

On re-examination—

    (a) a witness may be questioned about matters arising out of evidence given by the witness in cross-examination; and

    (b) other questions may not be put to the witness unless the court gives leave.

Division 5—Cross-examination

40. Witness called in error
A party is not to cross-examine a witness who has been called in error by another party and has not been questioned by that other party about a matter relevant to a question to be determined in the proceeding.

41. Improper questions
(1) The court must disallow an improper question or improper questioning put to a witness in cross-examination, or inform the witness that it need not be answered.
*****

(3) In this section, improper question or improper questioning means a question or a sequence of questions put to a witness that—
    (a) is misleading or confusing; or
    (b) is unduly annoying, harassing, intimidating, offensive, oppressive, humiliating or repetitive; or
    (c) is put to the witness in a manner or tone that is belittling, insulting or otherwise inappropriate; or
    (d) has no basis other than a stereotype (for example, a stereotype based on the witness's sex, race, culture, ethnicity, age or mental, intellectual or physical disability).
*****

(5) A question is not an improper question merely because—
    (a) the question challenges the truthfulness of the witness or the consistency or accuracy of any statement made by the witness; or
    (b) the question requires the witness to discuss a subject that could be considered distasteful to, or private by, the witness.

(6) A party may object to a question put to a witness on the ground that it is an improper question.

(7) However, the duty imposed on the court by this section applies whether or not an objection is raised to a particular question.

(8) A failure by the court to disallow a question under this section, or to inform the witness that it need not be answered, does not affect the admissibility in evidence of any answer given by the witness in response to the question.

    Notes- A person must not, without the express permission of a court, print or publish any question that the court has disallowed under this section— see section 195.

42. Leading questions

(1) A party may put a leading question to a witness in cross-examination unless the court disallows the question or directs the witness not to answer it.

(2) Without limiting the matters that the court may take into account in deciding whether to disallow the question or give such a direction, it is to take into account the extent to which—

    (a) evidence that has been given by the witness in examination in chief is unfavourable to the party who called the witness; and

    (b) the witness has an interest consistent with an interest of the cross-examiner; and

    (c) the witness is sympathetic to the party conducting the cross-examination, either generally or about a particular matter; and

    (d) the witness's age, or any mental, intellectual or physical disability to which the witness is subject, may affect the witness's answers.

(3) The court is to disallow the question, or direct the witness not to answer it, if the court is satisfied that the facts concerned would be better ascertained if leading questions were not used.

(4) This section does not limit the court's power to control leading questions.

43. Prior inconsistent statements of witnesses

(1) A witness may be cross-examined about a prior inconsistent statement alleged to have been made by the witness whether or not—

    (a) complete particulars of the statement have been given to the witness; or

    (b) a document containing a record of the statement has been shown to the witness.

(2) If, in cross-examination, a witness does not admit that he or she has made a prior inconsistent statement, the cross-examiner is not to adduce evidence of the statement otherwise than from the witness unless, in the cross-examination, the cross-examiner—

    (a) informed the witness of enough of the circumstances of the making of the statement to enable the witness to identify the statement; and

    (b) drew the witness's attention to so much of the statement as is inconsistent with the witness's evidence.

(3) For the purpose of adducing evidence of the statement, a party may re-open the party's case.

44. Previous representations of other persons

(1) Except as provided by this section, a cross-examiner must not question a witness about a previous representation alleged to have been made by a person other than the witness.

(2) A cross-examiner may question a witness about the representation and its contents if—

    (a) evidence of the representation has been admitted; or

    (b) the court is satisfied that it will be admitted.

(3) If subsection (2) does not apply and the representation is contained in a document, the document may only be used to question a witness as follows—

    (a) the document must be produced to the witness;

(b) if the document is a tape recording, or any other kind of document from which sounds are reproduced—the witness must be provided with the means (for example, headphones) to listen to the contents of the document without other persons present at the cross-examination hearing those contents;

(c) the witness must be asked whether, having examined (or heard) the contents of the document, the witness stands by the evidence that he or she has given;

(d) neither the cross-examiner nor the witness is to identify the document or disclose any of its contents.

(4) A document that is so used may be marked for identification.

45. Production of documents

(1) This section applies if a party is cross-examining or has cross-examined a witness about—

(a) a prior inconsistent statement alleged to have been made by the witness that is recorded in a document; or

(b) a previous representation alleged to have been made by another person that is recorded in a document.

(2) If the court so orders or if another party so requires, the party must produce—

(a) the document; or

(b) such evidence of the contents of the document as is available to the party—

to the court or to that other party.

(3) The court may—

(a) examine a document or evidence that has been so produced; and

(b) give directions as to its use; and

(c) admit it even if it has not been tendered by a party.

(4) Subsection (3) does not permit the court to admit a document or evidence that is not admissible because of Chapter 3.

(5) The mere production of a document to a witness who is being cross-examined does not give rise to a requirement that the cross-examiner tender the document.

46. Leave to recall witnesses

(1) The court may give leave to a party to recall a witness to give evidence about a matter raised by evidence adduced by another party, being a matter on which the witness was not cross-examined, if the evidence concerned has been admitted and—

(a) it contradicts evidence about the matter given by the witness in examination in chief; or

(b) the witness could have given evidence about the matter in examination in chief.

(2) A reference in this section to a matter raised by evidence adduced by another party includes a reference to an inference drawn from, or that the party intends to draw from, that evidence.

Part 2.2—Documents

47. Definitions

(1) A reference in this Part to a document in question is a reference to a document as to the contents of which it is sought to adduce evidence.

(2) A reference in this Part to a copy of a document in question includes a reference to a document that is not an exact copy of the document in question but that is identical to the document in question in all relevant respects.

48. Proof of contents of documents

(1) A party may adduce evidence of the contents of a document in question by tendering the document in question or by any one or more of the following methods—

(a) adducing evidence of an admission made by another party to the proceeding as to the contents of the document in question;

(b) tendering a document that—

(i) is or purports to be a copy of the document in question; and

(ii) has been produced, or purports to have been produced, by a device that reproduces the contents of documents;

(c) if the document in question is an article or thing by which words are recorded in such a way as to be capable of being reproduced as sound, or in which words are recorded in a code (including shorthand writing)— tendering a document that is or purports to be a transcript of the words;

(d) if the document in question is an article or thing on or in which information is stored in such a way that it cannot be used by the court unless a device is used to retrieve, produce or collate it—tendering a document that was or purports to have been produced by use of the device;

(e) tendering a document that—

(i) forms part of the records of or kept by a business (whether or not the business is still in existence); and

(ii) is or purports to be a copy of, or an extract from or a summary of, the document in question, or is or purports to be a copy of such an extract or summary;

(f) if the document in question is a public document—tendering a document that is or purports to be a copy of the document in question and that is or purports to have been printed—

(i) by a person authorised by or on behalf of the Government to print the document or by the Government Printer of the Commonwealth or by the government or official printer of another State or a Territory; or

(ii) by the authority of the Government or administration of the State, the Commonwealth, another State, a Territory or a foreign country; or

(iii) by authority of an Australian Parliament, a House of an Australian Parliament, a committee of such a House or a committee of an Australian Parliament.

(2) Subsection (1) applies to a document in question whether the document in question is available to the party or not.

(3) If the party adduces evidence of the contents of a document under subsection (1)(a), the evidence may only be used—

    (a) in respect of the party's case against the other party who made the admission concerned; or

    (b) in respect of the other party's case against the party who adduced the evidence in that way.

(4) A party may adduce evidence of the contents of a document in question that is not available to the party, or the existence and contents of which are not in issue in the proceeding, by—

    (a) tendering a document that is a copy of, or an extract from or summary of, the document in question; or

    (b) adducing from a witness evidence of the contents of the document in question.

        Notes-1. Clause 5 of Part 2 of the Dictionary is about the availability of documents…

49. Documents in foreign countries

No paragraph of section 48(1) (other than paragraph (a)) applies to a document that is in a foreign country unless—

    (a) the party who adduces evidence of the contents of the document in question has, not less than 28 days (or such other period as may be prescribed by the regulations or by rules of court) before the day on which the evidence is adduced, served on each other party a copy of the document proposed to be tendered; or

    (b) the court directs that it is to apply.

Note - Section 182 of the Commonwealth Act gives section 49 of the Commonwealth Act a wider application in relation to Commonwealth records and certain Commonwealth documents.

50. Proof of voluminous or complex documents

(1) The court may, on the application of a party, direct that the party may adduce evidence of the contents of 2 or more documents in question in the form of a summary if the court is satisfied that it would not otherwise be possible conveniently to examine the evidence because of the volume or complexity of the documents in question.

(2) The court may only make such a direction if the party seeking to adduce the evidence in the form of a summary has—

    (a) served on each other party a copy of the summary that discloses the name and address of the person who prepared the summary; and

    (b) given each other party a reasonable opportunity to examine or copy the documents in question.

(3) The opinion rule does not apply to evidence adduced in accordance with a direction under this section.

51. Original document rule abolished

The principles and rules of the common law that relate to the means of proving the contents of documents are abolished.

    Note - Section 182 of the Commonwealth Act gives the provisions of Part 2.2 of the Commonwealth Act a wider application in relation to Commonwealth records and certain Commonwealth documents.

Part 2.3—Other evidence

52. Adducing of other evidence not affected

This Act (other than this Part) does not affect the operation of any Australian law or rule of practice so far as it permits evidence to be adduced in a way other than by witnesses giving evidence or documents being tendered in evidence.

53. Views

(1) A judge may, on application, order that a demonstration, experiment or inspection be held.

(2) A judge is not to make an order unless he or she is satisfied that—

(a) the parties will be given a reasonable opportunity to be present; and

(b) the judge and, if there is a jury, the jury will be present.

(3) Without limiting the matters that the judge may take into account in deciding whether to make an order, the judge is to take into account the following—

(a) whether the parties will be present;

(b) whether the demonstration, experiment or inspection will, in the court's opinion, assist the court in resolving issues of fact or understanding the evidence;

(c) the danger that the demonstration, experiment or inspection might be unfairly prejudicial, might be misleading or confusing or might cause or result in undue waste of time;

(d) in the case of a demonstration—the extent to which the demonstration will properly reproduce the conduct or event to be demonstrated;

(e) in the case of an inspection—the extent to which the place or thing to be inspected has materially altered.

(4) The court (including, if there is a jury, the jury) is not to conduct an experiment in the course of its deliberations.

(5) This section does not apply in relation to the inspection of an exhibit by the court or, if there is a jury, by the jury.

54. Views to be evidence

The court (including, if there is a jury, the jury) may draw any reasonable inference from what it sees, hears or otherwise notices during a demonstration, experiment or inspection.

Chapter 3—Admissibility of evidence

Introductory Note

Outline of this Chapter

This Chapter is about whether evidence adduced in a proceeding is admissible.

Part 3.1 sets out the general inclusionary rule that relevant evidence is admissible.

Part 3.2 is about the exclusion of hearsay evidence, and exceptions to the hearsay rule.

Part 3.3 is about exclusion of opinion evidence, and exceptions to the opinion rule.

Part 3.4 is about admissions and the extent to which they are admissible as exceptions to the hearsay rule and the opinion rule.

Part 3.5 is about exclusion of certain evidence of judgments and convictions.

Part 3.6 is about exclusion of evidence of tendency or coincidence, and exceptions to the tendency rule and the coincidence rule.

Part 3.7 is about exclusion of evidence relevant only to credibility, and exceptions to the credibility rule.

Part 3.8 is about character evidence and the extent to which it is admissible as exceptions to the hearsay rule, the opinion rule, the tendency rule and the credibility rule.

Part 3.9 is about the requirements that must be satisfied before identification evidence is admissible.

Part 3.10 is about the various categories of privilege that may prevent evidence being adduced.

Part 3.11 provides for the discretionary and mandatory exclusion of evidence even if it would otherwise be admissible.

Chapter 3—Admissibility of evidence
(Diagram)

The following diagram shows how this Chapter applies to particular evidence—

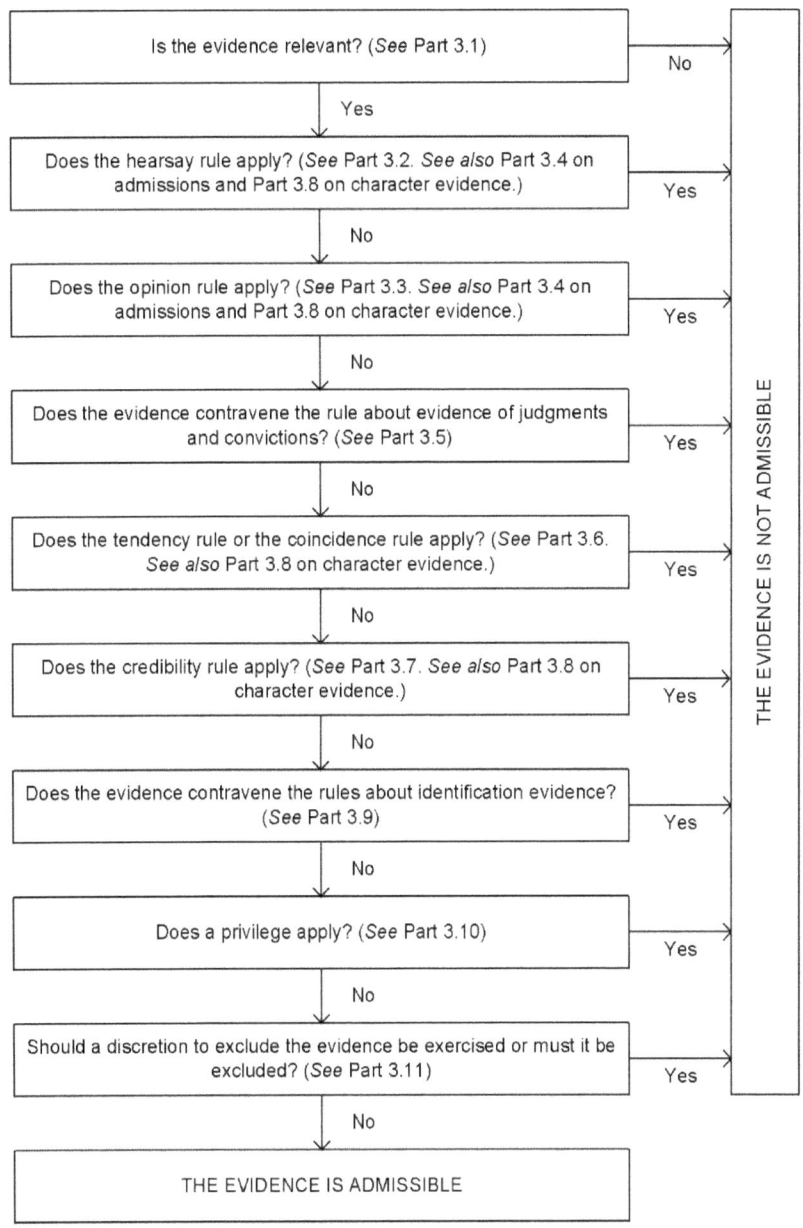

Part 3.1—Relevance

55. Relevant evidence

(1) The evidence that is relevant in a proceeding is evidence that, if it were accepted, could rationally affect (directly or indirectly) the assessment of the probability of the existence of a fact in issue in the proceeding.

(2) In particular, evidence is not taken to be irrelevant only because it relates only to—

(a) the credibility of a witness; or

(b) the admissibility of other evidence; or

(c) a failure to adduce evidence.

56. Relevant evidence to be admissible

(1) Except as otherwise provided by this Act, evidence that is relevant in a proceeding is admissible in the proceeding.

(2) Evidence that is not relevant in the proceeding is not admissible.

57. Provisional relevance

(1) If the determination of the question whether evidence adduced by a party is relevant depends on the court making another finding (including a finding that the evidence is what the party claims it to be), the court may find that the evidence is relevant—

(a) if it is reasonably open to make that finding; or

(b) subject to further evidence being admitted at a later stage of the proceeding that will make it reasonably open to make that finding.

(2) Without limiting subsection (1), if the relevance of evidence of an act done by a person depends on the court making a finding that the person and one or more other persons had, or were acting in furtherance of, a common purpose (whether to effect an unlawful conspiracy or as part of involvement in the commission of an offence or otherwise), the court may use the evidence itself in determining whether the common purpose existed.

Notes-2. Subdivision (1) of Division 1 of Part II of the Crimes Act 1958 deals with complicity in commission of offences.

58. Inferences as to relevance

(1) If a question arises as to the relevance of a document or thing, the court may examine it and may draw any reasonable inference from it, including an inference as to its authenticity or identity.

(2) Subsection (1) does not limit the matters from which inferences may properly be drawn.

Part 3.2—Hearsay
Division 1—The hearsay rule

59. The hearsay rule—exclusion of hearsay evidence

(1) Evidence of a previous representation made by a person is not admissible to prove the existence of a fact that it can reasonably be supposed that the person intended to assert by the representation.

(2) Such a fact is in this Part referred to as an asserted fact.

(2A) For the purposes of determining under subsection (1) whether it can reasonably be supposed that the person intended to assert a particular fact by the representation, the court may have regard to the circumstances in which the representation was made.

Notes-2.Specific exceptions to the hearsay rule are as follows—
- evidence relevant for a non-hearsay purpose (section 60)
- first-hand hearsay—
  - civil proceedings, if the maker of the representation is unavailable (section 63) or available (section 64)
  - criminal proceedings, if the maker of the representation is unavailable (section 65) or available (section 66)
  - contemporaneous statements about a person's health etc. (section 66A)
  - business records (section 69)
  - tags and labels (section 70)
  - electronic communications (section 71)
  - Aboriginal and Torres Strait Islander traditional laws and customs (section 72)
  - marriage, family history or family relationships (section 73)
  - public or general rights (section 74)
  - use of evidence in interlocutory proceedings (section 75)
  - admissions (section 81)
  - representations about employment or authority (section 87(2))
  - exceptions to the rule excluding evidence of judgments and convictions (section 92(3))
  - character of and expert opinion about an accused (sections 110 and 111).

Other provisions of this Act, or of other laws, may operate as further exceptions.

Examples

1. D is the accused in a sexual assault trial. W has made a statement to the police that X told W that X had seen D leave a night club with the victim shortly before the sexual assault is alleged to have occurred. Unless an exception to the hearsay rule applies, evidence of what X told W cannot be given at the trial.

2. P had told W that the handbrake on W's car did not work. Unless an exception to the hearsay rule applies, evidence of that statement cannot be given by P, W or anyone else to prove that the handbrake was defective.

3. W had bought a video cassette recorder and written down its serial number on a document. Unless an exception to the hearsay rule applies, the document is inadmissible to prove that a video cassette recorder later found in D's possession was the video cassette recorder bought by W.

60. Exception—evidence relevant for a non-hearsay purpose

(1) The hearsay rule does not apply to evidence of a previous representation that is admitted because it is relevant for a purpose other than proof of an asserted fact.

(2) This section applies whether or not the person who made the representation had personal knowledge of the asserted fact (within the meaning of section 62(2)).

Note

(3) However, this section does not apply in a criminal proceeding to evidence of an admission.

> **Note-**The admission might still be admissible under section 81 as an exception to the hearsay rule if it is "first-hand" hearsay—see section 82.

61. Exceptions to the hearsay rule dependant on competency

(1) This Part does not enable use of a previous representation to prove the existence of an asserted fact if, when the representation was made, the person who made it was not competent to give evidence about the fact because of section 13(1).

(2) This section does not apply to a contemporaneous representation made by a person about his or her health, feelings, sensations, intention, knowledge or state of mind.

> **Note-**For the admissibility of such contemporaneous representations, see section 66A.

(3) For the purposes of this section, it is presumed, unless the contrary is proved, that when the representation was made the person who made it was competent to give evidence about the asserted fact.

Division 2—"First-hand" hearsay

62. Restriction to "first-hand" hearsay

(1) A reference in this Division (other than in subsection (2)) to a previous representation is a reference to a previous representation that was made by a person who had personal knowledge of an asserted fact.

(2) A person has personal knowledge of the asserted fact if his or her knowledge of the fact was, or might reasonably be supposed to have been, based on something that the person saw, heard or otherwise perceived, other than a previous representation made by another person about the fact.

(3) For the purposes of section 66A, a person has personal knowledge of the asserted fact if it is a fact about the person's health, feelings, sensations, intention, knowledge or state of mind at the time the representation referred to in that section was made.

63. Exception—civil proceedings if maker not available

(1) This section applies in a civil proceeding if a person who made a previous representation is not available to give evidence about an asserted fact.

(2) The hearsay rule does not apply to—

    (a) evidence of the representation that is given by a person who saw, heard or otherwise perceived the representation being made; or

(b) a document so far as it contains the representation, or another representation to which it is reasonably necessary to refer in order to understand the representation.

Notes-1. Section 67 imposes notice requirements relating to this subsection.

64. Exception—civil proceedings if maker available

(1) This section applies in a civil proceeding if a person who made a previous representation is available to give evidence about an asserted fact.

(2) The hearsay rule does not apply to—

(a) evidence of the representation that is given by a person who saw, heard or otherwise perceived the representation being made; or

(b) a document so far as it contains the representation, or another representation to which it is reasonably necessary to refer in order to understand the representation—

if it would cause undue expense or undue delay, or would not be reasonably practicable, to call the person who made the representation to give evidence.

> **Note** - Section 67 imposes notice requirements relating to this subsection. Section 68 is about objections to notices that relate to this subsection.

(3) If the person who made the representation has been or is to be called to give evidence, the hearsay rule does not apply to evidence of the representation that is given by—

(a) that person; or

(b) a person who saw, heard or otherwise perceived the representation being made.

(4) A document containing a representation to which subsection (3) applies must not be tendered before the conclusion of the examination in chief of the person who made the representation, unless the court gives leave.

> **Note**- Clause 4 of Part 2 of the Dictionary is about the availability of persons.

65. Exception—criminal proceedings if maker not available

(1) This section applies in a criminal proceeding if a person who made a previous representation is not available to give evidence about an asserted fact.

(2) The hearsay rule does not apply to evidence of a previous representation that is given by a person who saw, heard or otherwise perceived the representation being made, if the representation—

(a) was made under a duty to make that representation or to make representations of that kind; or

(b) was made when or shortly after the asserted fact occurred and in circumstances that make it unlikely that the representation is a fabrication; or

(c) was made in circumstances that make it highly probable that the representation is reliable; or

(d) was—

(i) against the interests of the person who made it at the time it was made; and

(ii) made in circumstances that make it likely that the representation is reliable.

> **Note**-Section 67 imposes notice requirements relating to this subsection.

(3) The hearsay rule does not apply to evidence of a previous representation made in the course of giving evidence in an Australian or overseas proceeding if, in that proceeding, the accused in the proceeding to which this section is being applied—

(a) cross-examined the person who made the representation about it; or

(b) had a reasonable opportunity to cross-examine the person who made the representation about it.

> **Note**-Section 67 imposes notice requirements relating to this subsection.

(4) If there is more than one accused in the criminal proceeding, evidence of a previous representation that—

(a) is given in an Australian or overseas proceeding; and

(b) is admitted into evidence in the criminal proceeding because of subsection (3)—

cannot be used against an accused who did not cross-examine, and did not have a reasonable opportunity to cross-examine, the person about the representation.

(5) For the purposes of subsections (3) and (4), an accused is taken to have had a reasonable opportunity to cross-examine a person if the accused was not present at a time when the cross-examination of a person might have been conducted but—

(a) could reasonably have been present at that time; and

(b) if present could have cross-examined the person.

(6) Evidence of the making of a representation to which subsection (3) applies may be adduced by producing a transcript, or a recording, of the representation that is authenticated by—

(a) the person to whom, or the court or other body to which, the representation was made; or

(b) if applicable, the registrar or other proper officer of the court or other body to which the representation was made; or

(c) the person or body responsible for producing the transcript or recording.

(7) Without limiting subsection (2)(d), a representation is taken for the purposes of that subsection to be against the interests of the person who made it if it tends—

(a) to damage the person's reputation; or

(b) to show that the person has committed an offence for which the person has not been convicted; or

(c) to show that the person is liable in an action for damages.

(8) The hearsay rule does not apply to—

(a) evidence of a previous representation adduced by an accused if the evidence is given by a person who saw, heard or otherwise perceived the representation being made; or

(b) a document tendered as evidence by an accused so far as it contains a previous representation, or another representation to which it is reasonably necessary to refer in order to understand the representation.

> **Note**-Section 67 imposes notice requirements relating to this subsection.

(9) If evidence of a previous representation about a matter has been adduced by an accused and has been admitted, the hearsay rule does not apply to evidence of another representation about the matter that—

(a) is adduced by another party; and

(b) is given by a person who saw, heard or otherwise perceived the other representation being made.

> **Note**-Clause 4 of Part 2 of the Dictionary is about the availability of persons.

66. Exception—criminal proceedings if maker available

(1) This section applies in a criminal proceeding if a person who made a previous representation is available to give evidence about an asserted fact.

(2) The hearsay rule does not apply to evidence of the representation that is given by the person who made the representation or a person who saw, heard or otherwise perceived the representation being made if—

    (a) the person who made the representation has been or is to be called to give evidence; and

    (b) either—

        (i) when the representation was made, the occurrence of the asserted fact was fresh in the memory of the person who made the representation; or

        (ii) the person who made the representation is a victim of an offence to which the proceeding relates and was under the age of 18 years when the representation was made.

(2A) In determining whether the occurrence of the asserted fact was fresh in the memory of a person, the court may take into account all matters that it considers are relevant to the question, including—

    (a) the nature of the event concerned; and

    (b) the age and health of the person; and

    (c) the period of time between the occurrence of the asserted fact and the making of the representation.

(3) If a representation was made for the purpose of indicating the evidence that the person who made it would be able to give in an Australian or overseas proceeding, subsection (2) does not apply to evidence adduced by the prosecutor of the representation unless the representation concerns the identity of a person, place or thing.

(4) A document containing a representation to which subsection (2) applies must not be tendered before the conclusion of the examination in chief of the person who made the representation, unless the court gives leave.

    Note-Clause 4 of Part 2 of the Dictionary is about the availability of persons

66A. Exception—contemporaneous statements about a person's health etc.

The hearsay rule does not apply to evidence of a previous representation made by a person if the representation was a contemporaneous representation about the person's health, feelings, sensations, intention, knowledge or state of mind

67. Notice to be given

(1) Sections 63(2), 64(2) and 65(2), (3) and (8) do not apply to evidence adduced by a party unless that party has given reasonable notice in writing to each other party of the party's intention to adduce the evidence.

(2) Notices given under subsection (1) are to be given in accordance with any regulations or rules of court made for the purposes of this section.

(3) The notice must state—

(a) the particular provisions of this Division on which the party intends to rely in arguing that the hearsay rule does not apply to the evidence; and

(b) if section 64(2) is such a provision—the grounds, specified in that provision, on which the party intends to rely.

(4) Despite subsection (1), if notice has not been given, the court may, on the application of a party, direct that one or more of those subsections is to apply despite the party's failure to give notice.

(5) The direction—

(a) is subject to such conditions (if any) as the court thinks fit; and

(b) in particular, may provide that, in relation to specified evidence, the subsection or subsections concerned apply with such modifications as the court specifies.

68. Objections to tender of hearsay evidence in civil proceedings if maker available

(1) In a civil proceeding, if the notice discloses that it is not intended to call the person who made the previous representation concerned because it—

(a) would cause undue expense or undue delay; or

(b) would not be reasonably practicable—

a party may, not later than 21 days after notice has been given, object to the tender of the evidence, or of a specified part of the evidence.

(2) The objection is to be made by giving to each other party a written notice setting out the grounds on which the objection is made.

(3) The court may, on the application of a party, determine the objection at or before the hearing.

(4) If the objection is unreasonable, the court may order that, in any event, the party objecting is to bear the costs incurred by another party—

(a) in relation to the objection; and

(b in calling the person who made the representation to give evidence.

Division 3—Other exceptions to the hearsay rule
69. Exception—business records
(1) This section applies to a document that—
>   (a) either—
>>   (i) is or forms part of the records belonging to or kept by a person, body or organisation in the course of, or for the purposes of, a business; or
>>   (ii) at any time was or formed part of such a record; and
>   (b) contains a previous representation made or recorded in the document in the course of, or for the purposes of, the business.

(2) The hearsay rule does not apply to the document (so far as it contains the representation) if the representation was made—
>   (a) by a person who had or might reasonably be supposed to have had personal knowledge of the asserted fact; or
>   (b) on the basis of information directly or indirectly supplied by a person who had or might reasonably be supposed to have had personal knowledge of the asserted fact.

(3) Subsection (2) does not apply if the representation—
>   (a) was prepared or obtained for the purpose of conducting, or for or in contemplation of or in connection with, an Australian or overseas proceeding; or
>   (b) was made in connection with an investigation relating or leading to a criminal proceeding.

(4) If—
>   (a) the occurrence of an event of a particular kind is in question; and
>   (b) in the course of a business, a system has been followed of making and keeping a record of the occurrence of all events of that kind—
>>   the hearsay rule does not apply to evidence that tends to prove that there is no record kept, in accordance with that system, of the occurrence of the event.

(5) For the purposes of this section, a person is taken to have had personal knowledge of a fact if the person's knowledge of the fact was or might reasonably be supposed to have been based on what the person saw, heard or otherwise perceived (other than a previous representation made by a person about the fact).

>   **Note-**1. Sections 48, 49, 50, 146, 147 and 150(1) are relevant to the mode of proof, and authentication, of business records.

70. Exception—contents of tags, labels and writing
The hearsay rule does not apply to a tag or label attached to, or writing placed on, an object (including a document) if the tag or label or writing may reasonably be supposed to have been so attached or placed—
>   (a) in the course of a business; and
>   (b) for the purpose of describing or stating the identity, nature, ownership, destination, origin or weight of the object, or of the contents (if any) of the object.

>   **Note-**The Commonwealth Act has an additional subsection. It provides that the exception does not apply to Customs and Excise prosecutions. Section 5 of the Commonwealth Act extends the application of that subsection to proceedings in all Australian courts.

71. Exception—electronic communications

The hearsay rule does not apply to a representation contained in a document recording an electronic communication so far as the representation is a representation as to—

(a) the identity of the person from whom or on whose behalf the communication was sent; or

(b) the date on which or the time at which the communication was sent; or

(c) the destination of the communication or the identity of the person to whom the communication was addressed.

> **Notes**
>
> 1. Division 3 of Part 4.3 contains presumptions about electronic communications.
>
> 2. Section 182 of the Commonwealth Act gives section 71 of the Commonwealth Act a wider application in relation to Commonwealth records.
>
> 3. Electronic communication is defined in the Dictionary.

72. Exception—Aboriginal and Torres Strait Islander traditional laws and customs

The hearsay rule does not apply to evidence of a representation about the existence or non-existence, or the content, of the traditional laws and customs of an Aboriginal or Torres Strait Islander group.

> [Note-Section 72 formerly provided an exception for contemporaneous statements about a person's health etc. Such provision can now be found in section 66A.]

73. Exception—reputation as to relationships and age

(1) The hearsay rule does not apply to evidence of reputation concerning—

(a) whether a person was, at a particular time or at any time, a married person; or

(b) whether a man and a woman cohabiting at a particular time were married to each other at that time; or

(c) a person's age; or

(d) family history or a family relationship.

(2) In a criminal proceeding, subsection (1) does not apply to evidence adduced by an accused unless—

(a) it tends to contradict evidence of a kind referred to in subsection (1) that has been admitted; or

(b) the accused has given reasonable notice in writing to each other party of the intention of the accused to adduce the evidence.

(3) In a criminal proceeding, subsection (1) does not apply to evidence adduced by the prosecutor unless it tends to contradict evidence of a kind referred to in subsection (1) that has been admitted.

74. Exception—reputation of public or general rights

(1) The hearsay rule does not apply to evidence of reputation concerning the existence, nature or extent of a public or general right.

(2) In a criminal proceeding, subsection (1) does not apply to evidence adduced by the prosecutor unless it tends to contradict evidence of a kind referred to in subsection (1) that has been admitted.

75. Exception—interlocutory proceedings

In an interlocutory proceeding, the hearsay rule does not apply to evidence if the party who adduces it also adduces evidence of its source.

Part 3.3—Opinion

76. The opinion rule

Evidence of an opinion is not admissible to prove the existence of a fact about the existence of which the opinion was expressed.

> **Notes-1.** The Commonwealth Act and New South Wales Act include an additional subsection.
>
> 2. Specific exceptions to the opinion rule are as follows—
>   - summaries of voluminous or complex documents (section 50(3))
>   - evidence relevant otherwise than as opinion evidence (section 77)
>   - lay opinion (section 78)
>   - Aboriginal and Torres Strait Islander traditional laws and customs (section 78A)
>   - expert opinion (section 79)
>   - admissions (section 81)
>   - exceptions to the rule excluding evidence of judgments and convictions (section 92(3))
>   - character of and expert opinion about an accused (sections 110 and 111).
>
> Other provisions of this Act, or of other laws, may operate as further exceptions.

Examples

1. P sues D, her doctor, for the negligent performance of a surgical operation. Unless an exception to the opinion rule applies, P's neighbour, W, who had the same operation, cannot give evidence of his opinion that D had not performed the operation as well as his own.

2. P considers that electrical work that D, an electrician, has done for her is unsatisfactory. Unless an exception to the opinion rule applies, P cannot give evidence of her opinion that D does not have the necessary skills to do electrical work.

77. Exception—evidence relevant otherwise than as opinion evidence

The opinion rule does not apply to evidence of an opinion that is admitted because it is relevant for a purpose other than proof of the existence of a fact about the existence of which the opinion was expressed.

78. Exception—lay opinions

The opinion rule does not apply to evidence of an opinion expressed by a person if—

(a) the opinion is based on what the person saw, heard or otherwise perceived about a matter or event; and

(b) evidence of the opinion is necessary to obtain an adequate account or understanding of the person's perception of the matter or event.

78A. Exception—Aboriginal and Torres Strait Islander traditional laws and customs

The opinion rule does not apply to evidence of an opinion expressed by a member of an Aboriginal or Torres Strait Islander group about the existence or non-existence, or the content, of the traditional laws and customs of the group.

79. Exception—opinions based on specialised knowledge

(1) If a person has specialised knowledge based on the person's training, study or experience, the opinion rule does not apply to evidence of an opinion of that person that is wholly or substantially based on that knowledge.

(2) To avoid doubt, and without limiting subsection (1)—

(a) a reference in that subsection to specialised knowledge includes a reference to specialised knowledge of child development and child behaviour (including specialised knowledge of the impact of sexual abuse on children and their development and behaviour during and following the abuse); and

(b) a reference in that subsection to an opinion of a person includes, if the person has specialised knowledge of the kind referred to in paragraph (a), a reference to an opinion relating to either or both of the following—

(i) the development and behaviour of children generally;

(ii) the development and behaviour of children who have been victims of sexual offences, or offences similar to sexual offences.

80. Ultimate issue and common knowledge rules abolished

Evidence of an opinion is not inadmissible only because it is about—

(a) a fact in issue or an ultimate issue; or

(b) a matter of common knowledge.

Part 3.4—Admissions

Note-Admission is defined in the Dictionary.

81. Hearsay and opinion rules—exception for admissions and related representations

(1) The hearsay rule and the opinion rule do not apply to evidence of an admission.

(2) The hearsay rule and the opinion rule do not apply to evidence of a previous representation—

(a) that was made in relation to an admission at the time the admission was made, or shortly before or after that time; and

(b) to which it is reasonably necessary to refer in order to understand the admission.

> **Note**-Specific exclusionary rules relating to admissions are as follows—
>
> •evidence of admissions that is not first-hand (section 82)
>
> •use of admissions against third parties (section 83)
>
> •admissions influenced by violence and certain other conduct (section 84)
>
> •unreliable admissions of an accused (section 85)
>
> •records of oral questioning of an accused (section 86)

Example

D admits to W, his best friend, that he sexually assaulted V. In D's trial for the sexual assault, the prosecution may lead evidence from W—

(a) that D made the admission to W as proof of the truth of that admission; and

(b) that W formed the opinion that D was sane when he made the admission.

82. Exclusion of evidence of admissions that is not first-hand

Section 81 does not prevent the application of the hearsay rule to evidence of an admission unless—

(a) it is given by a person who saw, heard or otherwise perceived the admission being made; or

(b) it is a document in which the admission is made.

> **Note**-Section 60 does not apply in a criminal proceeding to evidence of an admission.

83. Exclusion of evidence of admissions as against third parties

(1) Section 81 does not prevent the application of the hearsay rule or the opinion rule to evidence of an admission in respect of the case of a third party.

(2) The evidence may be used in respect of the case of a third party if that party consents.

(3) Consent cannot be given in respect of part only of the evidence.

(4) In this section, third party means a party to the proceeding concerned, other than the party who—

(a) made the admission; or

(b) adduced the evidence.

84. Exclusion of admissions influenced by violence and certain other conduct

(1) Evidence of an admission is not admissible unless the court is satisfied that the admission, and the making of the admission, were not influenced by—

(a) violent, oppressive, inhuman or degrading conduct, whether towards the person who made the admission or towards another person; or

(b) a threat of conduct of that kind.

(2) Subsection (1) only applies if the party against whom evidence of the admission is adduced has raised in the proceeding an issue about whether the admission or its making were so influenced.

85. Criminal proceedings—reliability of admissions by accused

(1) This section applies only in a criminal proceeding and only to evidence of an admission made by an accused—

(a) to, or in the presence of, an investigating official who at that time was performing functions in connection with the investigation of the commission, or possible commission, of an offence; or

(b) as a result of an act of another person who was, and who the accused knew or reasonably believed to be, capable of influencing the decision whether a prosecution of the accused should be brought or should be continued.

(2) Evidence of the admission is not admissible unless the circumstances in which the admission was made were such as to make it unlikely that the truth of the admission was adversely affected.

(3) Without limiting the matters that the court may take into account for the purposes of subsection (2), it is to take into account—

(a) any relevant condition or characteristic of the person who made the admission, including age, personality and education and any mental, intellectual or physical disability to which the person is or appears to be subject; and

(b) if the admission was made in response to questioning—

(i) the nature of the questions and the manner in which they were put; and

(ii) the nature of any threat, promise or other inducement made to the person questioned.

86. Exclusion of records of oral questioning

(1) This section applies only in a criminal proceeding and only if an oral admission was made by an accused to an investigating official in response to a question put or a representation made by the official.

(2) A document prepared by or on behalf of the official is not admissible to prove the contents of the question, representation or response unless the accused has acknowledged that the document is a true record of the question, representation or response.

(3) The acknowledgement must be made by signing, initialling or otherwise marking the document.

(4) In this section, document does not include—

    (a) a sound recording, or a transcript of a sound recording; or

    (b) a recording of visual images and sounds, or a transcript of the sounds so recorded.

        Note-See also sections 83 and 84 of the Criminal Procedure Act 2009 which relate to the admissibility of evidence in the absence of an accused in a summary hearing.

87. Admissions made with authority

(1) For the purpose of determining whether a previous representation made by a person is also taken to be an admission by a party, the court is to admit the representation if it is reasonably open to find that—

    (a) when the representation was made, the person had authority to make statements on behalf of the party in relation to the matter with respect to which the representation was made; or

    (b) when the representation was made, the person was an employee of the party, or had authority otherwise to act for the party, and the representation related to a matter within the scope of the person's employment or authority; or

    (c) the representation was made by the person in furtherance of a common purpose (whether lawful or not) that the person had with the party or one or more persons including the party.

(2) For the purposes of this section, the hearsay rule does not apply to a previous representation made by a person that tends to prove—

    (a) that the person had authority to make statements on behalf of another person in relation to a matter; or

    (b) that the person was an employee of another person or had authority otherwise to act for another person; or

    (c) the scope of the person's employment or authority.

88. Proof of admissions

For the purpose of determining whether evidence of an admission is admissible, the court is to find that a particular person made the admission if it is reasonably open to find that he or she made the admission.

89. Evidence of silence

(1) In a criminal proceeding, an inference unfavourable to a party must not be drawn from evidence that the party or another person failed or refused—

    (a) to answer one or more questions; or

    (b) to respond to a representation—

    put or made to the party or other person by an investigating official who at that time was performing functions in connection with the investigation of the commission, or possible commission, of an offence.

(2) Evidence of that kind is not admissible if it can only be used to draw such an inference.

(3) Subsection (1) does not prevent use of the evidence to prove that the party or other person failed or refused to answer the question or to respond to the representation if the failure or refusal is a fact in issue in the proceeding.

(4) In this section, inference includes—

    (a) an inference of consciousness of guilt; or

    (b) an inference relevant to a party's credibility.

90. Discretion to exclude admissions

In a criminal proceeding, the court may refuse to admit evidence of an admission, or refuse to admit the evidence to prove a particular fact, if—

    (a) the evidence is adduced by the prosecution; and

    (b) having regard to the circumstances in which the admission was made, it would be unfair to an accused to use the evidence.

    Note-Part 3.11 contains other exclusionary discretions that are applicable to admissions.

Part 3.5—Evidence of judgments and convictions

91. Exclusion of evidence of judgments and convictions

(1) Evidence of the decision, or of a finding of fact, in an Australian or overseas proceeding is not admissible to prove the existence of a fact that was in issue in that proceeding.

(2) Evidence that, under this Part, is not admissible to prove the existence of a fact may not be used to prove that fact even if it is relevant for another purpose.

    Note-Section 178 (Convictions, acquittals and other judicial proceedings) provides for certificate evidence of decisions.

92. Exceptions

(1) Section 91(1) does not prevent the admission or use of evidence of the grant of probate, letters of administration or a similar order of a court to prove—

    (a) the death, or date of death, of a person; or

    (b) the due execution of a testamentary document.

(2) In a civil proceeding, section 91(1) does not prevent the admission or use of evidence that a party, or a person through or under whom a party claims, has been convicted of an offence, not being a conviction—

    (a) in respect of which a review or appeal (however described) has been instituted but not finally determined; or

    (b) that has been quashed or set aside; or

    (c) in respect of which a pardon has been given.

(3) The hearsay rule and the opinion rule do not apply to evidence of a kind referred to in this section.

93. Savings

This Part does not affect the operation of—
(a) a law that relates to the admissibility or effect of evidence of a conviction tendered in a proceeding (including a criminal proceeding) for defamation; or
(b) a judgment in rem; or
(c) the law relating to res judicata or issue estoppel.

Part 3.6—Tendency and coincidence

Note-See also Division 2 of Part 4 of the Jury Directions Act 2015.

94. Application

(1) This Part does not apply to evidence that relates only to the credibility of a witness.
(2) This Part does not apply so far as a proceeding relates to bail or sentencing.
(3) This Part does not apply to evidence of—
    (a) the character, reputation or conduct of a person; or
    (b) a tendency that a person has or had—
        if that character, reputation, conduct or tendency is a fact in issue.

95. Use of evidence for other purposes

(1) Evidence that under this Part is not admissible to prove a particular matter must not be used to prove that matter even if it is relevant for another purpose.
(2) Evidence that under this Part cannot be used against a party to prove a particular matter must not be used against the party to prove that matter even if it is relevant for another purpose.

96. Failure to act

A reference in this Part to doing an act includes a reference to failing to do that act.

97. The tendency rule

(1) Evidence of the character, reputation or conduct of a person, or a tendency that a person has or had, is not admissible to prove that a person has or had a tendency (whether because of the person's character or otherwise) to act in a particular way, or to have a particular state of mind unless—
    (a)the party seeking to adduce the evidence gave reasonable notice in writing to each other party of the party's intention to adduce the evidence; and
    (b)the court thinks that the evidence will, either by itself or having regard to other evidence adduced or to be adduced by the party seeking to adduce the evidence, have significant probative value.
(2) Subsection (1)(a) does not apply if—
    (a)the evidence is adduced in accordance with any directions made by the court under section 100; or
    (b)the evidence is adduced to explain or contradict tendency evidence adduced by another party.
        Note-The tendency rule is subject to specific exceptions concerning character of and expert opinion about an accused (sections 110 and 111). Other provisions of this Act, or of other laws, may operate as further exceptions.

98. The coincidence rule

(1) Evidence that 2 or more events occurred is not admissible to prove that a person did a particular act or had a particular state of mind on the basis that, having regard to any similarities in the events or the circumstances in which they occurred, or any similarities in both the events and the circumstances in which they occurred, it is improbable that the events occurred coincidentally unless—

(a) the party seeking to adduce the evidence gave reasonable notice in writing to each other party of the party's intention to adduce the evidence; and

(b) the court thinks that the evidence will, either by itself or having regard to other evidence adduced or to be adduced by the party seeking to adduce the evidence, have significant probative value.

   Note-One of the events referred to in subsection (1) may be an event the occurrence of which is a fact in issue in the proceeding.

(2) Subsection (1)(a) does not apply if—

(a) the evidence is adduced in accordance with any directions made by the court under section 100; or

(b) the evidence is adduced to explain or contradict coincidence evidence adduced by another party.

   Note-Other provisions of this Act, or of other laws, may operate as exceptions to the coincidence rule.

99. Requirements for notices

Notices given under section 97 or 98 are to be given in accordance with any regulations or rules of court made for the purposes of this section.

100. Court may dispense with notice requirements

(1) The court may, on the application of a party, direct that the tendency rule is not to apply to particular tendency evidence despite the party's failure to give notice under section 97.

(2) The court may, on the application of a party, direct that the coincidence rule is not to apply to particular coincidence evidence despite the party's failure to give notice under section 98.

(3) The application may be made either before or after the time by which the party would, apart from this section, be required to give, or to have given, the notice.

(4) In a civil proceeding, the party's application may be made without notice of it having been given to one or more of the other parties.

(5) The direction—

(a) is subject to such conditions (if any) as the court thinks fit; and

(b) may be given either at or before the hearing.

(6) Without limiting the court's power to impose conditions under this section, those conditions may include one or more of the following—

(a) a condition that the party give notice of its intention to adduce the evidence to a specified party, or to each other party other than a specified party;

(b) a condition that the party give such notice only in respect of specified tendency evidence, or all tendency evidence that the party intends to adduce other than specified tendency evidence;

(c) a condition that the party give such notice only in respect of specified coincidence evidence, or all coincidence evidence that the party intends to adduce other than specified coincidence evidence.

101. Further restrictions on tendency evidence and coincidence evidence adduced by prosecution

(1) This section only applies in a criminal proceeding and so applies in addition to sections 97 and 98.

(2) Tendency evidence about an accused, or coincidence evidence about an accused, that is adduced by the prosecution cannot be used against the accused unless the probative value of the evidence substantially outweighs any prejudicial effect it may have on the accused.

(3) This section does not apply to tendency evidence that the prosecution adduces to explain or contradict tendency evidence adduced by the accused.

(4) This section does not apply to coincidence evidence that the prosecution adduces to explain or contradict coincidence evidence adduced by the accused.

Part 3.7—Credibility
Division 1—Credibility evidence

101A. Credibility evidence

Credibility evidence, in relation to a witness or other person, is evidence relevant to the credibility of the witness or person that—

(a) is relevant only because it affects the assessment of the credibility of the witness or person; or

(b) is relevant—

(i) because it affects the assessment of the credibility of the witness or person; and

(ii) for some other purpose for which it is not admissible, or cannot be used, because of a provision of Parts 3.2 to 3.6.

Notes-1 Sections 60 and 77 will not affect the application of paragraph (b), because they cannot apply to evidence that is yet to be admitted.

Division 2—Credibility of witnesses

102. The credibility rule

Credibility evidence about a witness is not admissible.

Notes-1. Specific exceptions to the credibility rule are as follows—
•evidence adduced in cross-examination (sections 103 and 104)
•evidence in rebuttal of denials (section 106)
•evidence to re-establish credibility (section 108)
•evidence of persons with specialised knowledge (section 108C)
•character of accused persons (section 110)

Other provisions of this Act, or of other laws, may operate as further exceptions.

2. Sections 108A and 108B deal with the admission of credibility evidence about a person who has made a previous representation but is not a witness.

103. Exception—cross-examination as to credibility
(1) The credibility rule does not apply to evidence adduced in cross-examination of a witness if the evidence could substantially affect the assessment of the credibility of the witness.
(2) Without limiting the matters to which the court may have regard for the purposes of subsection (1), it is to have regard to—
    (a) whether the evidence tends to prove that the witness knowingly or recklessly made a false representation when the witness was under an obligation to tell the truth; and
    (b) the period that has elapsed since the acts or events to which the evidence relates were done or occurred.

104. Further protections—cross-examination as to credibility
(1) This section applies only to credibility evidence in a criminal proceeding and so applies in addition to section 103.
(2) An accused must not be cross-examined about a matter that is relevant to the assessment of the credibility of the accused, unless the court gives leave.
(3) Despite subsection (2), leave is not required for cross-examination by the prosecutor about whether the accused—
    (a) is biased or has a motive to be untruthful; or
    (b) is, or was, unable to be aware of or recall matters to which his or her evidence relates; or
    (c) has made a prior inconsistent statement.
(4) Leave must not be given for cross-examination by the prosecutor under subsection (2) unless evidence adduced by the accused has been admitted that—
    (a) tends to prove that a witness called by the prosecutor has a tendency to be untruthful; and
    (b) is relevant solely or mainly to the witness's credibility.
(5) A reference in subsection (4) to evidence does not include a reference to evidence of conduct in relation to—
    (a) the events in relation to which the accused is being prosecuted; or
    (b) the investigation of the offence for which the accused is being prosecuted.
(6) Leave is not to be given for cross-examination by another accused unless—
    (a) the evidence that the accused to be cross-examined has given includes evidence adverse to the accused seeking leave to cross-examine; and
    (b) that evidence has been admitted.

105. Further protections—accused making unsworn statements *****

106. Exception—rebutting denials by other evidence

(1) The credibility rule does not apply to evidence that is relevant to a witness's credibility and that is adduced otherwise than from the witness if—

    (a) in cross-examination of the witness—

        (i) the substance of the evidence was put to the witness; and

        (ii) the witness denied, or did not admit or agree to, the substance of the evidence; and

    (b) the court gives leave to adduce the evidence.

(2) Leave under subsection (1)(b) is not required if the evidence tends to prove that the witness—

    (a) is biased or has a motive for being untruthful; or

    (b) has been convicted of an offence, including an offence against the law of a foreign country; or

    (c) has made a prior inconsistent statement; or

    (d) is, or was, unable to be aware of matters to which his or her evidence relates; or

    (e) has knowingly or recklessly made a false representation while under an obligation, imposed by or under an Australian law or a law of a foreign country, to tell the truth.

107. Exception—application of certain provisions to makers of representations *****

108. Exception—re-establishing credibility

(1) The credibility rule does not apply to evidence adduced in re-examination of a witness.

(2) *****

    Note-The Commonwealth Act previously included a subsection referring to section 105 of that Act.

(3) The credibility rule does not apply to evidence of a prior consistent statement of a witness if—

    (a) evidence of a prior inconsistent statement of the witness has been admitted; or

    (b) it is or will be suggested (either expressly or by implication) that evidence given by the witness has been fabricated or re-constructed (whether deliberately or otherwise) or is the result of a suggestion—

    and the court gives leave to adduce the evidence of the prior consistent statement.

Division 3—Credibility of persons who are not witnesses

108A. Admissibility of evidence of credibility of person who has made a previous representation

(1) If—

(a) evidence of a previous representation has been admitted in a proceeding; and

(b) the person who made the representation has not been called, and will not be called, to give evidence in the proceeding—

credibility evidence about the person who made the representation is not admissible unless the evidence could substantially affect the assessment of the person's credibility.

(2) Without limiting the matters to which the court may have regard for the purposes of subsection (1), it is to have regard to—

(a) whether the evidence tends to prove that the person who made the representation knowingly or recklessly made a false representation when the person was under an obligation to tell the truth; and

(b) the period that elapsed between the doing of the acts or the occurrence of the events to which the representation related and the making of the representation.

108B. Further protections—previous representations of an accused who is not a witness

(1) This section applies only in a criminal proceeding and so applies in addition to section 108A.

(2) If the person referred to in that section is an accused, the credibility evidence is not admissible unless the court gives leave.

(3) Despite subsection (2), leave is not required if the evidence is about whether the accused—

(a) is biased or has a motive to be untruthful; or

(b) is, or was, unable to be aware of or recall matters to which his or her previous representation relates; or

(c) has made a prior inconsistent statement.

(4) The prosecution must not be given leave under subsection (2) unless evidence adduced by the accused has been admitted that—

(a) tends to prove that a witness called by the prosecution has a tendency to be untruthful; and

(b) is relevant solely or mainly to the witness's credibility.

(5) A reference in subsection (4) to evidence does not include a reference to evidence of conduct in relation to—

(a) the events in relation to which the accused is being prosecuted; or

(b) the investigation of the offence for which the accused is being prosecuted.

(6) Another accused must not be given leave under subsection (2) unless the previous representation of the accused that has been admitted includes evidence adverse to the accused seeking leave.

Division 4—Persons with specialised knowledge

108C. Exception—evidence of persons with specialised knowledge
(1) The credibility rule does not apply to evidence given by a person concerning the credibility of another witness if—
    (a) the person has specialised knowledge based on the person's training, study or experience; and
    (b) the evidence is evidence of an opinion of the person that—
        (i) is wholly or substantially based on that knowledge; and
        (ii) could substantially affect the assessment of the credibility of the witness; and
    (c) the court gives leave to adduce the evidence.
(2) To avoid doubt, and without limiting subsection (1)—
    (a) a reference in that subsection to specialised knowledge includes a reference to specialised knowledge of child development and child behaviour (including specialised knowledge of the impact of sexual abuse on children and their behaviour during and following the abuse); and
    (b) a reference in that subsection to an opinion of a person includes, if the person has specialised knowledge of that kind, a reference to an opinion relating to either or both of the following—
        (i) the development and behaviour of children generally;
        (ii) the development and behaviour of children who have been victims of sexual offences, or offences similar to sexual offences.

Part 3.8—Character

109. Application
This Part applies only in a criminal proceeding.

110. Evidence about character of an accused
(1) The hearsay rule, the opinion rule, the tendency rule and the credibility rule do not apply to evidence adduced by an accused to prove (directly or by implication) that the accused is, either generally or in a particular respect, a person of good character.
(2) If evidence adduced to prove (directly or by implication) that an accused is generally a person of good character has been admitted, the hearsay rule, the opinion rule, the tendency rule and the credibility rule do not apply to evidence adduced to prove (directly or by implication) that the accused is not generally a person of good character.
(3) If evidence adduced to prove (directly or by implication) that an accused is a person of good character in a particular respect has been admitted, the hearsay rule, the opinion rule, the tendency rule and the credibility rule do not apply to evidence adduced to prove (directly or by implication) that the accused is not a person of good character in that respect.

111. Evidence about character of co-accused

(1) The hearsay rule and the tendency rule do not apply to evidence of the character of an accused if—

(a) the evidence is evidence of an opinion about the accused adduced by another accused; and

(b) the person whose opinion it is has specialised knowledge based on the person's training, study or experience; and

(c) the opinion is wholly or substantially based on that knowledge.

(2) If such evidence has been admitted, the hearsay rule, the opinion rule and the tendency rule do not apply to evidence adduced to prove that that evidence should not be accepted.

112. Leave required to cross-examine about character of accused or co-accused

An accused must not be cross-examined about matters arising out of evidence of a kind referred to in this Part unless the court gives leave.

Part 3.9—Identification evidence

Note-Identification evidence is defined in the Dictionary

113. Application of Part

This Part applies only in a criminal proceeding.

114. Exclusion of visual identification evidence

(1) In this section, visual identification evidence means identification evidence relating to an identification based wholly or partly on what a person saw but does not include picture identification evidence.

(2) Visual identification evidence adduced by the prosecutor is not admissible unless—

(a) an identification parade that included the accused was held before the identification was made; or

(b) it would not have been reasonable to have held such a parade; or

(c) the accused refused to take part in such a parade—

and the identification was made without the person who made it having been intentionally influenced to identify the accused.

(3) Without limiting the matters that may be taken into account by the court in determining whether it was reasonable to hold an identification parade, it is to take into account—

(a) the kind of offence, and the gravity of the offence, concerned; and

(b) the importance of the evidence; and

(c) the practicality of holding an identification parade having regard, among other things—

(i) if the accused failed to cooperate in the conduct of the parade—to the manner and extent of, and the reason (if any) for, the failure; and

(ii) in any case—to whether the identification was made at or about the time of the commission of the offence; and

(d) the appropriateness of holding an identification parade having regard, among other things, to the relationship (if any) between the accused and the person who made the identification.

(4) It is presumed that it would not have been reasonable to have held an identification parade if it would have been unfair to the accused for such a parade to have been held.

(5) If—

(a) the accused refused to take part in an identification parade unless an Australian legal practitioner acting for the accused, or another person chosen by the accused, was present while it was being held; and

(b) there were, at the time when the parade was to have been conducted, reasonable grounds to believe that it was not reasonably practicable for such an Australian legal practitioner or person to be present—

it is presumed that it would not have been reasonable to have held an identification parade at that time.

(6) In determining whether it was reasonable to have held an identification parade, the court is not to take into account the availability of pictures or photographs that could be used in making identifications.

115. Exclusion of evidence of identification by pictures

(1) In this section, picture identification evidence means identification evidence relating to an identification made wholly or partly by the person who made the identification examining pictures kept for the use of police officers.

(2) Picture identification evidence adduced by the prosecutor is not admissible if the pictures examined suggest that they are pictures of persons in police custody.

(3) Subject to subsection (4), picture identification evidence adduced by the prosecutor is not admissible if—

(a) when the pictures were examined, the accused was in the custody of a police officer of the police force investigating the commission of the offence with which the accused has been charged; and

(b) the picture of the accused that was examined was made before the accused was taken into that police custody.

(4) Subsection (3) does not apply if—

(a) the appearance of the accused had changed significantly between the time when the offence was committed and the time when the accused was taken into that custody; or

(b) it was not reasonably practicable to make a picture of the accused after the accused was taken into that custody.

(5) Picture identification evidence adduced by the prosecutor is not admissible if, when the pictures were examined, the accused was in the custody of a police officer of the police force investigating the commission of the offence with which the accused has been charged, unless—

(a) the accused refused to take part in an identification parade; or

(b) the appearance of the accused had changed significantly between the time when the offence was committed and the time when the accused was taken into that custody; or

(c) it would not have been reasonable to have held an identification parade that included the accused.

(6) Sections 114(3), (4), (5) and (6) apply in determining, for the purposes of subsection (5)(c) of this section, whether it would have been reasonable to have held an identification parade.

(7) If picture identification evidence adduced by the prosecutor is admitted into evidence, the judge must, on the request of the accused—

(a) if the picture of the accused was made after the accused was taken into that custody—inform the jury that the picture was made after the accused was taken into that custody; or

(b) otherwise—warn the jury that they must not assume that the accused has a criminal record or has previously been charged with an offence.

> Note-Division 4 of Part 4 of the Jury Directions Act 2015 also deals with warnings about identification evidence.

(8) This section does not render inadmissible picture identification evidence adduced by the prosecutor that contradicts or qualifies picture identification evidence adduced by the accused.

(9) This section applies in addition to section 114.

(10) In this section—

(a) a reference to a picture includes a reference to a photograph; and

(b) a reference to making a picture includes a reference to taking a photograph.

116. Directions to jury *****

> Note- Division 4 of Part 4 of the Jury Directions Act 2015 contains provisions relating to identification evidence that apply in criminal trials.

Part 3.10—Privileges
Division 1—Client legal privilege

117. Definitions
(1) In this Division—

client includes the following—

(a) a person or body who engages a lawyer to provide legal services or who employs a lawyer (including under a contract of service);

(b) an employee or agent of a client;

(c) an employer of a lawyer if the employer is—

(i) the Commonwealth or a State or Territory; or

(ii) a body established by a law of the Commonwealth or a State or Territory;

(d) if, under a law of a State or Territory relating to persons of unsound mind, a manager, committee or person (however described) is for the time being acting in respect of the person, estate or property of a client—a manager, committee or person so acting;

(e) if a client has died—a personal representative of the client;

(f) a successor to the rights and obligations of a client, being rights and obligations in respect of which a confidential communication was made;

confidential communication means a communication made in such circumstances that, when it was made—

(a) the person who made it; or

(b) the person to whom it was made—

was under an express or implied obligation not to disclose its contents, whether or not the obligation arises under law;

confidential document means a document prepared in such circumstances that, when it was prepared—

(a) the person who prepared it; or

(b) the person for whom it was prepared—

was under an express or implied obligation not to disclose its contents, whether or not the obligation arises under law;

lawyer means—

(a) an Australian lawyer; and

(b) a non-participant registered foreign lawyer; and

(c) a foreign lawyer or a natural person who, under the law of a foreign country, is permitted to engage in legal practice in that country; and

(d) an employee or agent of a lawyer referred to in paragraph (a), (b) or (c);

party includes the following—

(a) an employee or agent of a party;

(b) if, under a law of a State or Territory relating to persons of unsound mind, a manager, committee or person (however described) is for the time being acting in respect of the person, estate or property of a party—a manager, committee or person so acting;

(c) if a party has died—a personal representative of the party;

(d) a successor to the rights and obligations of a party, being rights and obligations in respect of which a confidential communication was made.

(2) A reference in this Division to the commission of an act includes a reference to a failure to act.

118. Legal advice
Evidence is not to be adduced if, on objection by a client, the court finds that adducing the evidence would result in disclosure of—
>   (a) a confidential communication made between the client and a lawyer; or
>   (b) a confidential communication made between 2 or more lawyers acting for the client; or
>   (c) the contents of a confidential document (whether delivered or not) prepared by the client, lawyer or another person—

for the dominant purpose of the lawyer, or one or more of the lawyers, providing legal advice to the client.

119. Litigation
Evidence is not to be adduced if, on objection by a client, the court finds that adducing the evidence would result in disclosure of—
>   (a) a confidential communication between the client and another person, or between a lawyer acting for the client and another person, that was made; or
>   (b) the contents of a confidential document (whether delivered or not) that was prepared—

for the dominant purpose of the client being provided with professional legal services relating to an Australian or overseas proceeding (including the proceeding before the court), or an anticipated or pending Australian or overseas proceeding, in which the client is or may be, or was or might have been, a party.

120. Unrepresented parties
(1) Evidence is not to be adduced if, on objection by a party who is not represented in the proceeding by a lawyer, the court finds that adducing the evidence would result in disclosure of—
(a) a confidential communication between the party and another person; or
>   (b) the contents of a confidential document (whether delivered or not) that was prepared, either by or at the direction or request of, the party—

for the dominant purpose of preparing for or conducting the proceeding.
(2) *****

121. Loss of client legal privilege—generally
(1) This Division does not prevent the adducing of evidence relevant to a question concerning the intentions, or competence in law, of a client or party who has died.
(2) This Division does not prevent the adducing of evidence if, were the evidence not adduced, the court would be prevented, or it could reasonably be expected that the court would be prevented, from enforcing an order of an Australian court.
(3) This Division does not prevent the adducing of evidence of a communication or document that affects a right of a person.

122. Loss of client legal privilege—consent and related matters

(1) This Division does not prevent the adducing of evidence given with the consent of the client or party concerned.

(2) Subject to subsection (5), this Division does not prevent the adducing of evidence if the client or party concerned has acted in a way that is inconsistent with the client or party objecting to the adducing of the evidence because it would result in a disclosure of a kind referred to in section 118, 119 or 120.

(3) Without limiting subsection (2), a client or party is taken to have so acted if—

(a) the client or party knowingly and voluntarily disclosed the substance of the evidence to another person; or

(b) the substance of the evidence has been disclosed with the express or implied consent of the client or party.

(4) The reference in subsection (3)(a) to a knowing and voluntary disclosure does not include a reference to a disclosure by a person who was, at the time of the disclosure, an employee or agent of the client or party or of a lawyer of the client or party unless the employee or agent was authorised by the client, party or lawyer to make the disclosure.

(5) A client or party is not taken to have acted in a manner inconsistent with the client or party objecting to the adducing of the evidence merely because—

(a) the substance of the evidence has been disclosed—

(i) in the course of making a confidential communication or preparing a confidential document; or

(ii) as a result of duress or deception; or

(iii) under compulsion of law; or

(iv) if the client or party is a body established by, or a person holding an office under, an Australian law—to the Minister, or the Minister of the Commonwealth, the State or Territory, administering the law, or part of the law, under which the body is established or the office is held; or

(b) of a disclosure by a client to another person if the disclosure concerns a matter in relation to which the same lawyer is providing, or is to provide, professional legal services to both the client and the other person; or

(c) of a disclosure to a person with whom the client or party had, at the time of the disclosure, a common interest relating to the proceeding or an anticipated or pending proceeding in an Australian court or a foreign court.

(6) This Division does not prevent the adducing of evidence of a document that a witness has used to try to revive the witness's memory about a fact or opinion or has used as mentioned in section 32 (Attempts to revive memory in court) or 33 (Evidence given by police officers).

123. Loss of client legal privilege—accused

In a criminal proceeding, this Division does not prevent an accused from adducing evidence unless it is evidence of—

(a) a confidential communication made between an associated accused and a lawyer acting for that person in connection with the prosecution of that person; or

(b) the contents of a confidential document prepared by an associated accused or by a lawyer acting for that person in connection with the prosecution of that person.

124. Loss of client legal privilege—joint clients

(1) This section only applies to a civil proceeding in connection with which 2 or more parties have, before the commencement of the proceeding, jointly retained a lawyer in relation to the same matter.

(2) This Division does not prevent one of those parties from adducing evidence of—

(a) a communication made by any one of them to the lawyer; or

(b) the contents of a confidential document prepared by or at the direction or request of any one of them—

in connection with that matter.

125. Loss of client legal privilege—misconduct

(1) This Division does not prevent the adducing of evidence of—

(a) a communication made or the contents of a document prepared by a client or lawyer (or both), or a party who is not represented in the proceeding by a lawyer, in furtherance of the commission of a fraud or an offence or the commission of an act that renders a person liable to a civil penalty; or

(b) a communication or the contents of a document that the client or lawyer (or both), or the party, knew or ought reasonably to have known was made or prepared in furtherance of a deliberate abuse of a power.

(2) For the purposes of this section, if the commission of the fraud, offence or act, or the abuse of power, is a fact in issue and there are reasonable grounds for finding that—

(a) the fraud, offence or act, or the abuse of power, was committed; and

(b) a communication was made or document prepared in furtherance of the commission of the fraud, offence or act or the abuse of power—

the court may find that the communication was so made or the document so prepared.

(3) In this section, power means a power conferred by or under an Australian law.

126. Loss of client legal privilege—related communications and documents

If, because of the application of section 121, 122, 123, 124 or 125, this Division does not prevent the adducing of evidence of a communication or the contents of a document, those sections do not prevent the adducing of evidence of another communication or document if it is reasonably necessary to enable a proper understanding of the communication or document.

Example

A lawyer advises his client to understate her income for the previous year to evade taxation because of her potential tax liability "as set out in my previous letter to you dated 11 August 1994". In proceedings against the taxpayer for tax evasion, evidence of the contents of the letter dated 11 August 1994 may be admissible (even if that letter would otherwise be privileged) to enable a proper understanding of the second letter.

Division 1A—Professional confidential relationship privilege

Division 1B—Sexual assault communications privilege

Division 1C—Journalist privilege

126J. Definitions

(1) In this Division—

informant means a person who gives information to a journalist in the normal course of the journalist's work in the expectation that the information may be published in a news medium;

journalist means a person engaged in the profession or occupation of journalism in connection with the publication of information, comment, opinion or analysis in a news medium;

news medium means a medium for the dissemination to the public or a section of the public of news and observations on news.

(2) For the purpose of the definition of journalist, in determining if a person is engaged in the profession or occupation of journalism regard must be had to the following factors—

(a) whether a significant proportion of the person's professional activity involves—

(i) the practice of collecting and preparing information having the character of news or current affairs; or

(ii) commenting or providing opinion on or analysis of news or current affairs—

for dissemination in a news medium;

(b) whether information, having the character of news or current affairs, collected and prepared by the person is regularly published in a news medium;

(c) whether the person's comments or opinion on or analysis of news or current affairs is regularly published in a news medium;

(d) whether, in respect of the publication of—

(i) any information collected or prepared by the person; or

(ii) any comment or opinion on or analysis of news or current affairs by the person—

the person or the publisher of the information, comment, opinion or analysis is accountable to comply (through a complaints process) with recognised journalistic or media professional standards or codes of practice.

126K. Journalist privilege relating to identity of informant

(1) If a journalist, in the course of the journalist's work, has promised an informant not to disclose the informant's identity, neither the journalist nor his or her employer is compellable to give evidence that would disclose the identity of the informant or enable that identity to be ascertained.

(2) The court may, on the application of a party, order that subsection (1) is not to apply if it is satisfied that, having regard to the issues to be determined in the proceeding, the public interest in the disclosure of the identity of the informant outweighs—

(a) any likely adverse effect of the disclosure on the informant or any other person; and

(b) the public interest in the communication of facts and opinion to the public by the news media and, accordingly also, in the ability of the news media to access sources of facts.

(3) An order under subsection (2) may be made subject to such terms and conditions (if any) as the court thinks fit.

Division 2—Other privileges

127. Religious confessions

(1) A person who is or was a member of the clergy of any church or religious denomination is entitled to refuse to divulge that a religious confession was made, or the contents of a religious confession made, to the person when a member of the clergy.

(2) Subsection (1) does not apply—

(a) if the communication involved in the religious confession was made for a criminal purpose; or

(b) in a proceeding for an offence against section 184 of the Children, Youth and Families Act 2005; or

(c) in a proceeding for an offence against section 327(2) of the Crimes Act 1958.

(3) This section applies even if an Act provides—

(a) that the rules of evidence do not apply or that a person or body is not bound by the rules of evidence; or

(b) that a person is not excused from answering any question or producing any document or other thing on the ground of privilege or any other ground.

(4) In this section, religious confession means a confession made by a person to a member of the clergy in the member's professional capacity according to the ritual of the church or religious denomination concerned.

128. Privilege in respect of self-incrimination in other proceedings

(1) This section applies if a witness objects to giving particular evidence, or evidence on a particular matter, on the ground that the evidence may tend to prove that the witness—

(a) has committed an offence against or arising under an Australian law or a law of a foreign country; or

(b) is liable to a civil penalty.

(2) The court must determine whether or not there are reasonable grounds for the objection.

(3) Subject to subsection (4), if the court determines that there are reasonable grounds for the objection, the court is not to require the witness to give the evidence, and is to inform the witness—

(a) that the witness need not give the evidence unless required by the court to do so under subsection (4); and

(b) that the court will give a certificate under this section if—

(i) the witness willingly gives the evidence without being required to do so under subsection (4); or

(ii) the witness gives the evidence after being required to do so under subsection (4); and

(c) of the effect of such a certificate.

(4) The court may require the witness to give the evidence if the court is satisfied that—

(a) the evidence does not tend to prove that the witness has committed an offence against or arising under, or is liable to a civil penalty under, a law of a foreign country; and

(b) the interests of justice require that the witness give the evidence.

(5) If the witness either willingly gives the evidence without being required to do so under subsection (4), or gives it after being required to do so under that subsection, the court must cause the witness to be given a certificate under this section in respect of the evidence.

(6) The court is also to cause a witness to be given a certificate under this section if—

(a) the objection has been overruled; and

(b) after the evidence has been given, the court finds that there were reasonable grounds for the objection.

(7) In any proceeding in a Victorian court or before any person or body authorised by a law of this State, or by consent of parties, to hear, receive and examine evidence—

(a) evidence given by a person in respect of which a certificate under this section has been given; and

(b) evidence of any information, document or thing obtained as a direct or indirect consequence of the person having given evidence—

cannot be used against the person. However, this does not apply to a criminal proceeding in respect of the falsity of the evidence."

(8) Subsection (7) has effect despite any challenge, review, quashing or calling into question on any ground of the decision to give, or the validity of, the certificate concerned.

(9) If an accused in a criminal proceeding for an offence is given a certificate under this section, subsection (7) does not apply in a proceeding that is a retrial of the accused for the same offence or a trial of the accused for an offence arising out of the same facts that gave rise to that offence.

(10) In a criminal proceeding, this section does not apply in relation to the giving of evidence by an accused, being evidence that the accused—

    (a) did an act the doing of which is a fact in issue; or

    (b) had a state of mind the existence of which is a fact in issue.

(11) A reference in this section to doing an act includes a reference to failing to act.

(12) If a person has been given a certificate under a prescribed State or Territory provision in respect of evidence given by a person in a proceeding in a State or Territory court, the certificate has the same effect, in a proceeding to which this subsection applies, as if it had been given under this section.

(13) For the purposes of subsection (12), a prescribed State or Territory provision is a provision of a law of a State or Territory declared by the regulations to be a prescribed State or Territory provision for the purposes of that subsection.

(14) Subsection (12) applies to a proceeding in relation to which this Act applies because of section 4, other than a proceeding for an offence against a law of the Commonwealth or for the recovery of a civil penalty under a law of the Commonwealth.

> **Notes-**1 Bodies corporate cannot claim this privilege. See section 187.
> 2. Clause 3 of Part 2 of the Dictionary sets out what is a civil penalty.
> 3. Section 128(12) to (14) of the Commonwealth Act gives effect to certificates in relation to self-incriminating evidence under this Act in proceedings in federal and ACT courts and in prosecutions for Commonwealth and ACT offences.

128A. Privilege in respect of self-incrimination—exception for certain orders etc.

(1) In this section—

disclosure order means an order made by a Victorian court in a civil proceeding requiring a person to disclose information, as part of, or in connection with a freezing or search order under the Rules of the Supreme Court but does not include an order made by a court under the Proceeds of Crime Act 2002 of the Commonwealth or the Confiscation Act 1997;

relevant person means a person to whom a disclosure order is directed.

(2) If a relevant person objects to complying with a disclosure order on the grounds that some or all of the information required to be disclosed may tend to prove that the person—

(a) has committed an offence against or arising under an Australian law or a law of a foreign country; or

(b) is liable to a civil penalty—

the person must—

(c) disclose so much of the information required to be disclosed to which no objection is taken; and

(d) prepare an affidavit containing so much of the information required to be disclosed to which objection is taken (the privilege affidavit) and deliver it to the court in a sealed envelope; and

(e) file and serve on each other party a separate affidavit setting out the basis of the objection.

(3) The sealed envelope containing the privilege affidavit must not be opened except as directed by the court.

(4) The court must determine whether or not there are reasonable grounds for the objection.

(5) Subject to subsection (6), if the court finds that there are reasonable grounds for the objection, the court must not require the information contained in the privilege affidavit to be disclosed and must return it to the relevant person.

(6) If the court is satisfied that—

(a) any information disclosed in the privilege affidavit may tend to prove that the relevant person has committed an offence against or arising under, or is liable to a civil penalty under, an Australian law; and

(b) the information does not tend to prove that the relevant person has committed an offence against or arising under, or is liable to a civil penalty under, a law of a foreign country; and

(c) the interests of justice require the information to be disclosed—

the court may make an order requiring the whole or any part of the privilege affidavit containing information of the kind referred to in paragraph (a) to be filed and served on the parties.

(7) If the whole or any part of the privilege affidavit is disclosed (including by order under subsection (6)), the court must cause the relevant person to be given a certificate in respect of the information referred to in subsection (6)(a).

(8) In any proceeding in a Victorian court—

(a) evidence of information disclosed by a relevant person in respect of which a certificate has been given under this section; and

(b) evidence of any information, document or thing obtained as a direct result or indirect consequence of the relevant person having disclosed that information—

cannot be used against the person. However, this does not apply to a criminal proceeding in respect of the falsity of the evidence concerned.

(9) Subsection (8) does not prevent the use against the relevant person of any information disclosed by a document—

(a) that is an annexure or exhibit to a privilege affidavit prepared by the person in response to a disclosure order; and

(b) that was in existence before the order was made.

(10) Subsection (8) has effect despite any challenge, review, quashing or calling into question on any ground of the decision to give, or the validity of, the certificate concerned.

(11) If a person has been given a certificate under a prescribed State or Territory provision in respect of information of a kind referred to in subsection (6)(a), the certificate has the same effect, in a proceeding to which this subsection applies, as if it had been given under this section.

(12) For the purposes of subsection (11), a prescribed State or Territory provision is a provision of a law of a State or Territory declared by the regulations to be a prescribed State or Territory provision for the purposes of that subsection.

(13) Subsection (11) applies to a proceeding in relation to which this Act applies because of section 4, other than a proceeding for an offence against a law of the Commonwealth or for the recovery of a civil penalty under a law of the Commonwealth.

Division 3—Evidence excluded in the public interest

129. Exclusion of evidence of reasons for judicial etc. decisions

(1) Evidence of the reasons for a decision made by a person who is—

(a) a judge in an Australian or overseas proceeding; or

(b) an arbitrator in respect of a dispute that has been submitted to the person, or to the person and one or more other persons, for arbitration— or the deliberations of a person so acting in relation to such a decision, must not be given by the person, or a person who was, in relation to the proceeding or arbitration, under the direction or control of that person.

(2) Such evidence must not be given by tendering as evidence a document prepared by such a person.

(3) This section does not prevent the admission or use, in a proceeding, of published reasons for a decision.

(4) In a proceeding, evidence of the reasons for a decision made by a member of a jury in another Australian or overseas proceeding, or of the deliberations of a member of a jury in relation to such a decision, must not be given by any of the members of that jury.

(5) This section does not apply in a proceeding that is—

(a) a prosecution for one or more of the following offences—

(i) attempt to pervert the course of justice;

(ii) perverting the course of justice;

(iii) subornation of perjury;

(iv) embracery;

(v) bribery of public official;

(vi) misconduct in public office;

(vii) an offence against section 52A of the Summary Offences Act 1966 (Offence to harass witness etc.);

(viii) an offence against section 66 (Offences by officials) or 78 (Confidentiality of jury's deliberations) of the Juries Act 2000;

(ix) an offence connected with an offence mentioned in subparagraphs (i) to (viii), including an offence of conspiring to commit such an offence; or

(b) in respect of a contempt of a court; or

(c) by way of appeal from, or judicial review of, a judgment, decree, order or sentence of a court; or

(d) by way of review of an arbitral award; or

(e) a civil proceeding in respect of an act of a judicial officer or arbitrator that was, and that was known at the time by the judicial officer or arbitrator to be, outside the scope of the matters in relation to which the judicial officer or arbitrator had authority to act.

130. Exclusion of evidence of matters of state

(1) If the public interest in admitting into evidence information or a document that relates to matters of state is outweighed by the public interest in preserving secrecy or confidentiality in relation to the information or document, the court may direct that the information or document not be adduced as evidence.

(2) The court may give such a direction either on its own initiative or on the application of any person (whether or not the person is a party).

(3) In deciding whether to give such a direction, the court may inform itself in any way it thinks fit.

(4) Without limiting the circumstances in which information or a document may be taken for the purposes of subsection (1) to relate to matters of state, the information or document is taken for the purposes of that subsection to relate to matters of state if adducing it as evidence would—

(a) prejudice the security, defence or international relations of Australia; or

(b) damage relations between the Commonwealth and a State or between 2 or more States; or

(c) prejudice the prevention, investigation or prosecution of an offence; or

(d) prejudice the prevention or investigation of, or the conduct of proceedings for recovery of civil penalties brought with respect to, other contraventions of the law; or

(e) disclose, or enable a person to ascertain, the existence or identity of a confidential source of information relating to the enforcement or administration of a law of the Commonwealth or a State; or

(f) prejudice the proper functioning of the government of the Commonwealth or a State.

(5) Without limiting the matters that the court may take into account for the purposes of subsection (1), it is to take into account the following matters—

(a) the importance of the information or the document in the proceeding;

(b) if the proceeding is a criminal proceeding—whether the party seeking to adduce evidence of the information or document is an accused or the prosecutor;

(c) the nature of the offence, cause of action or defence to which the information or document relates, and the nature of the subject matter of the proceeding;

(d) the likely effect of adducing evidence of the information or document, and the means available to limit its publication;

(e) whether the substance of the information or document has already been published;

(f) if the proceeding is a criminal proceeding and the party seeking to adduce evidence of the information or document is an accused—whether the direction is to be made subject to the condition that the prosecution be stayed.

(6) A reference in this section to a State includes a reference to a Territory.

131. Exclusion of evidence of settlement negotiations

(1) Evidence is not to be adduced of—

(a) a communication that is made between persons in dispute, or between one or more persons in dispute and a third party, in connection with an attempt to negotiate a settlement of the dispute; or

(b) a document (whether delivered or not) that has been prepared in connection with an attempt to negotiate a settlement of a dispute.

(2) Subsection (1) does not apply if—

(a) the persons in dispute consent to the evidence being adduced in the proceeding concerned or, if any of those persons has tendered the communication or document in evidence in another Australian or overseas proceeding, all the other persons so consent; or

(b) the substance of the evidence has been disclosed with the express or implied consent of all the persons in dispute; or

(c) the substance of the evidence has been partly disclosed with the express or implied consent of the persons in dispute, and full disclosure of the evidence is reasonably necessary to enable a proper understanding of the other evidence that has already been adduced; or

(d) the communication or document included a statement to the effect that it was not to be treated as confidential; or

(e) the evidence tends to contradict or to qualify evidence that has already been admitted about the course of an attempt to settle the dispute; or

(f) the proceeding in which it is sought to adduce the evidence is a proceeding to enforce an agreement between the persons in dispute to settle the dispute, or a proceeding in which the making of such an agreement is in issue; or

(g) evidence that has been adduced in the proceeding, or an inference from evidence that has been adduced in the proceeding, is likely to mislead the court unless evidence of the communication or document is adduced to contradict or to qualify that evidence; or

(h) the communication or document is relevant to determining liability for costs; or

(i) making the communication, or preparing the document, affects a right of a person; or

(j) the communication was made, or the document was prepared, in furtherance of the commission of a fraud or an offence or the commission of an act that renders a person liable to a civil penalty; or

(k) one of the persons in dispute, or an employee or agent of such a person, knew or ought reasonably to have known that the communication was made, or the document was prepared, in furtherance of a deliberate abuse of a power.

(3) For the purposes of subsection (2)(j), if commission of the fraud, offence or act is a fact in issue and there are reasonable grounds for finding that—

(a) the fraud, offence or act was committed; and

(b) a communication was made or document prepared in furtherance of the commission of the fraud, offence or act—

the court may find that the communication was so made or the document so prepared.

(4) For the purposes of subsection (2)(k), if—

(a) the abuse of power is a fact in issue; and

(b) there are reasonable grounds for finding that a communication was made or document prepared in furtherance of the abuse of power—

the court may find that the communication was so made or the document was so prepared.

(5) In this section—

(a) a reference to a dispute is a reference to a dispute of a kind in respect of which relief may be given in an Australian or overseas proceeding; and

(b) a reference to an attempt to negotiate the settlement of a dispute does not include a reference to an attempt to negotiate the settlement of a criminal proceeding or an anticipated criminal proceeding; and

(c) a reference to a communication made by a person in dispute includes a reference to a communication made by an employee or agent of such a person; and

(d) a reference to the consent of a person in dispute includes a reference to the consent of an employee or agent of such a person, being an employee or agent who is authorised so to consent; and

(e) a reference to commission of an act includes a reference to a failure to act.

(6) In this section, power means a power conferred by or under an Australian law.

Division 4—General

131A. Application of Part to preliminary proceedings of courts

(1) If—

(a) a person is required by a disclosure requirement to give information, or to produce a document, which would result in the disclosure of a communication, a document or its contents or other information of a kind referred to in Division 1, 1C or 3; and

(b) the person objects to giving that information or providing that document—

the court must determine the objection by applying the provisions of this Part (other than sections 123 and 128) with any necessary modifications as if the objection to giving information or producing the document were an objection to the giving or adducing of evidence.

(2) In this section, disclosure requirement means a process or order of a court that requires the disclosure of information or a document and includes the following—

(a) a summons or subpoena to produce documents or give evidence;

(b) pre-trial discovery;

(c) non-party discovery;

(d) interrogatories;

(e) a notice to produce;

(f) a request to produce a document under Division 1 of Part 4.6;

(g) a search warrant.

132. Court to inform of rights to make applications and objections

If it appears to the court that a witness or a party may have grounds for making an application or objection under a provision of this Part, the court must satisfy itself (if there is a jury, in the absence of the jury) that the witness or party is aware of the effect of that provision.

133. Court may inspect etc. documents

If a question arises under this Part relating to a document, the court may order that the document be produced to it and may inspect the document for the purpose of determining the question.

134. Inadmissibility of evidence that must not be adduced or given

Evidence that, because of this Part, must not be adduced or given in a proceeding is not admissible in the proceeding.

Part 3.11—Discretionary and mandatory exclusions

135. General discretion to exclude evidence

The court may refuse to admit evidence if its probative value is substantially outweighed by the danger that the evidence might—
  (a) be unfairly prejudicial to a party; or
  (b) be misleading or confusing; or
  (c) cause or result in undue waste of time; or
  (d) unnecessarily demean the deceased in a criminal proceeding for a homicide offence.

> **Note**-This section does not limit evidence of family violence that may be adduced under Part IC of the Crimes Act 1958.

136. General discretion to limit use of evidence

The court may limit the use to be made of evidence if there is a danger that a particular use of the evidence might—
  (a) be unfairly prejudicial to a party; or
  (b) be misleading or confusing.

137. Exclusion of prejudicial evidence in criminal proceedings

In a criminal proceeding, the court must refuse to admit evidence adduced by the prosecutor if its probative value is outweighed by the danger of unfair prejudice to the accused.

138. Exclusion of improperly or illegally obtained evidence

(1) Evidence that was obtained—

    (a) improperly or in contravention of an Australian law; or

    (b) in consequence of an impropriety or of a contravention of an Australian law—

is not to be admitted unless the desirability of admitting the evidence outweighs the undesirability of admitting evidence that has been obtained in the way in which the evidence was obtained.

(2) Without limiting subsection (1), evidence of an admission that was made during or in consequence of questioning, and evidence obtained in consequence of the admission, is taken to have been obtained improperly if the person conducting the questioning—

    (a) did, or omitted to do, an act in the course of the questioning even though he or she knew or ought reasonably to have known that the act or omission was likely to impair substantially the ability of the person being questioned to respond rationally to the questioning; or

    (b) made a false statement in the course of the questioning even though he or she knew or ought reasonably to have known that the statement was false and that making the false statement was likely to cause the person who was being questioned to make an admission.

(3) Without limiting the matters that the court may take into account under subsection (1), it is to take into account—

    (a) the probative value of the evidence; and

    (b) the importance of the evidence in the proceeding; and

    (c) the nature of the relevant offence, cause of action or defence and the nature of the subject-matter of the proceeding; and

    (d) the gravity of the impropriety or contravention; and

    (e) whether the impropriety or contravention was deliberate or reckless; and

    (f) whether the impropriety or contravention was contrary to or inconsistent with a right of a person recognised by the International Covenant on Civil and Political Rights; and

    (g) whether any other proceeding (whether or not in a court) has been or is likely to be taken in relation to the impropriety or contravention; and

    (h) the difficulty (if any) of obtaining the evidence without impropriety or contravention of an Australian law.

        Note-The International Covenant on Civil and Political Rights is set out in Schedule 2 to the Human Rights and Equal Opportunity Commission Act 1986 of the Commonwealth.

139. Cautioning of persons

(1) For the purposes of section 138(1)(a), evidence of a statement made or an act done by a person during questioning is taken to have been obtained improperly if—

(a) the person was under arrest for an offence at the time; and

(b) the questioning was conducted by an investigating official who was at the time empowered, because of the office that he or she held, to arrest the person; and

(c) before starting the questioning the investigating official did not caution the person that the person does not have to say or do anything but that anything the person does say or do may be used in evidence.

(2) For the purposes of section 138(1)(a), evidence of a statement made or an act done by a person during questioning is taken to have been obtained improperly if—

(a) the questioning was conducted by an investigating official who did not have the power to arrest the person; and

(b) the statement was made, or the act was done, after the investigating official formed a belief that there was sufficient evidence to establish that the person has committed an offence; and

(c) the investigating official did not, before the statement was made or the act was done, caution the person that the person does not have to say or do anything but that anything the person does say or do may be used in evidence.

(3) The caution must be given in, or translated into, a language in which the person is able to communicate with reasonable fluency, but need not be given in writing unless the person cannot hear adequately.

(4) Subsections (1), (2) and (3) do not apply so far as any Australian law requires the person to answer questions put by, or do things required by, the investigating official.

(5) A reference in subsection (1) to a person who is under arrest includes a reference to a person who is in the company of an investigating official for the purpose of being questioned, if—

(a) the official believes that there is sufficient evidence to establish that the person has committed an offence that is to be the subject of the questioning; or

(b) the official would not allow the person to leave if the person wished to do so; or

(c) the official has given the person reasonable grounds for believing that the person would not be allowed to leave if he or she wished to do so.

(6) A person is not treated as being under arrest only because of subsection (5) if—

(a) the official is performing functions in relation to persons or goods entering or leaving Australia and the official does not believe the person has committed an offence against a law of the Commonwealth; or

(b) the official is exercising a power under an Australian law to detain and search the person or to require the person to provide information or to answer questions.

Chapter 4—Proof

Introductory Note

Outline of this Chapter

This Chapter is about the proof of matters in a proceeding.

Part 4.1 is about the standard of proof in civil proceedings and in criminal proceedings.

Part 4.2 is about matters that do not require proof in a proceeding.

Part 4.3 makes easier the proof of the matters dealt with in that Part.

Part 4.4 is about requirements that evidence be corroborated.

Part 4.5 requires judges to warn juries about the potential unreliability of certain kinds of evidence.

Part 4.6 sets out procedures for proving certain other matters.

Part 4.1—Standard of proof

140. Civil proceedings—standard of proof

(1) In a civil proceeding, the court must find the case of a party proved if it is satisfied that the case has been proved on the balance of probabilities.

(2) Without limiting the matters that the court may take into account in deciding whether it is so satisfied, it is to take into account—

    (a) the nature of the cause of action or defence; and

    (b) the nature of the subject-matter of the proceeding; and

    (c) the gravity of the matters alleged.

141. Criminal proceedings—standard of proof

(1) In a criminal proceeding, the court is not to find the case of the prosecution proved unless it is satisfied that it has been proved beyond reasonable doubt.

(2) In a criminal proceeding, the court is to find the case of an accused proved if it is satisfied that the case has been proved on the balance of probabilities.

142. Admissibility of evidence—standard of proof

(1) Except as otherwise provided by this Act, in any proceeding the court is to find that the facts necessary for deciding—

    (a) a question whether evidence should be admitted or not admitted, whether in the exercise of a discretion or not; or

    (b) any other question arising under this Act—

    have been proved if it is satisfied that they have been proved on the balance of probabilities.

(2) In determining whether it is so satisfied, the matters that the court must take into account include—

    (a) the importance of the evidence in the proceeding; and

    (b) the gravity of the matters alleged in relation to the question.

Part 4.2—Judicial notice

143. Matters of law

(1) Proof is not required about the provisions and coming into operation (in whole or in part) of—

(a) an Act, an Imperial Act in force in Australia, a Commonwealth Act, an Act of another State or an Act or Ordinance of a Territory; or

(b) a regulation, rule or by-law made, or purporting to be made, under such an Act or Ordinance; or

(c) a proclamation or order of the Governor-General, the Governor of a State or the Administrator or Executive of a Territory made, or purporting to be made, under such an Act or Ordinance; or

(d) an instrument of a legislative character (for example, a rule of court) made, or purporting to be made, under such an Act or Ordinance, being an instrument that is required by or under a law to be published, or the making of which is required by or under a law to be notified, in any government or official gazette (by whatever name called).

(2) A judge may inform himself or herself about those matters in any way that the judge thinks fit.

(3) A reference in this section to an Act, being an Act of an Australian Parliament, includes a reference to a private Act passed by that Parliament.

Note-Section 5 of the Commonwealth Act extends the operation of the equivalent Commonwealth section to proceedings in all Australian courts.

144. Matters of common knowledge

(1) Proof is not required about knowledge that is not reasonably open to question and is—

(a) common knowledge in the locality in which the proceeding is being held or generally; or

(b) capable of verification by reference to a document the authority of which cannot reasonably be questioned.

(2) The judge may acquire knowledge of that kind in any way the judge thinks fit.

(3) The court (including, if there is a jury, the jury) is to take knowledge of that kind into account.

(4) The judge is to give a party such opportunity to make submissions, and to refer to relevant information, relating to the acquiring or taking into account of knowledge of that kind as is necessary to ensure that the party is not unfairly prejudiced.

145. Certain Crown certificates

This Part does not exclude the application of the principles and rules of the common law and of equity relating to the effect of a certificate given by or on behalf of the Crown with respect to a matter of international affairs.

Part 4.3—Facilitation of proof
Division 1—General

146. Evidence produced by processes, machines and other devices

(1) This section applies to a document or thing—

    (a) that is produced wholly or partly by a device or process; and

    (b) that is tendered by a party who asserts that, in producing the document or thing, the device or process has produced a particular outcome.

(2) If it is reasonably open to find that the device or process is one that, or is of a kind that, if properly used, ordinarily produces that outcome, it is presumed (unless evidence sufficient to raise doubt about the presumption is adduced) that, in producing the document or thing on the occasion in question, the device or process produced that outcome.

Example

It would not be necessary to call evidence to prove that a photocopier normally produced complete copies of documents and that it was working properly when it was used to photocopy a particular document.

147. Documents produced by processes, machines and other devices in the course of business

(1) This section applies to a document—

    (a) that is produced wholly or partly by a device or process; and

    (b) that is tendered by a party who asserts that, in producing the document, the device or process has produced a particular outcome.

(2) If—

    (a) the document is, or was at the time it was produced, part of the records of, or kept for the purposes of, a business (whether or not the business is still in existence); and

    (b) the device or process is or was at that time used for the purposes of the business—

it is presumed (unless evidence sufficient to raise doubt about the presumption is adduced) that, in producing the document on the occasion in question, the device or process produced that outcome.

(3) Subsection (2) does not apply to the contents of a document that was produced—

    (a) for the purpose of conducting, or for or in contemplation of or in connection with, an Australian or overseas proceeding; or

    (b) in connection with an investigation relating or leading to a criminal proceeding.

148. Evidence of certain acts of justices, Australian lawyers and notaries public

It is presumed, unless the contrary is proved, that a document was attested or verified by, or signed or acknowledged before, a justice of the peace, Australian lawyer or notary public, if—

    (a) an Australian law requires, authorises or permits it to be attested, verified, signed or acknowledged by a justice of the peace, an Australian lawyer or a notary public, as the case may be; and

    (b) it purports to have been so attested, verified, signed or acknowledged.

149. Attestation of documents

It is not necessary to adduce the evidence of an attesting witness to a document (not being a testamentary document) to prove that the document was signed or attested as it purports to have been signed or attested.

150. Seals and signatures

(1) If the imprint of a seal appears on a document and purports to be the imprint of—
    (a) the Public Seal of the State; or
    (b) a Royal Great Seal; or
    (c) the Great Seal of Australia; or
    (d) another seal of the Commonwealth; or
    (e) a seal of another State, a Territory or a foreign country; or
    (f) the seal of a body (including a court or a tribunal), or a body corporate, established by or under Royal Charter or by an Australian law or the law of a foreign country—
    it is presumed, unless the contrary is proved, that the imprint is the imprint of that seal, and the document was duly sealed as it purports to have been sealed.
(2) If the imprint of a seal appears on a document and purports to be the imprint of the seal of an office holder, it is presumed, unless the contrary is proved, that—
(a) the imprint is the imprint of that seal; and
(b) the document was duly sealed by the office holder acting in his or her official capacity; and
(c) the office holder held the relevant office when the document was sealed.
(3) If a document purports to have been signed by an office holder in his or her official capacity, it is presumed, unless the contrary is proved, that—
(a) the document was signed by the office holder acting in that capacity; and
(b) the office holder held the relevant office when the document was signed.
(4) In this section, office holder means—
(a) the Sovereign; or
(b) the Governor-General; or
(c) the Governor of a State; or
(d) the Administrator of a Territory; or
(e) a person holding any other office under an Australian law or a law of a foreign country.
(5) This section extends to documents sealed, and documents signed, before the commencement of this section.

> **Notes**-3. See also section 142 of the Evidence (Miscellaneous Provisions) Act 1958 (Forgery, using etc. false documents an indictable offence).

151. Seals of bodies established under State law *****

152. Documents produced from proper custody

If a document that is or purports to be more than 20 years old is produced from proper custody, it is presumed, unless the contrary is proved, that—
    (a) the document is the document that it purports to be; and
    (b) if it purports to have been executed or attested by a person—it was duly executed or attested by that person.

Division 2—Matters of official record

153. Gazettes and other official documents

(1) It is presumed, unless the contrary is proved, that a document purporting—

(a) to be any government or official gazette (by whatever name called) of this State, the Commonwealth, another State, a Territory or a foreign country; or

(b) to have been printed by the Government Printer of this State, or by the government or official printer of the Commonwealth or of a State or Territory; or

(c) to have been printed by authority of the government or administration of this State, the Commonwealth, another State, a Territory or a foreign country—

is what it purports to be and was published on the day on which it purports to have been published.

(2) If—

(a) there is produced to a court—

(i) a copy of any government or official gazette (by whatever name called) of this State, the Commonwealth, another State, a Territory or a foreign country; or

(ii) a document that purports to have been printed by the Government Printer of this State, or by the government or official printer of the Commonwealth or of a State or Territory; or

(iii) a document that purports to have been printed by authority of the government or administration of this State, the Commonwealth, another State, a Territory or a foreign country; and

(b) the doing of an act—

(i) by the Governor-General or by the Governor of a State or the Administrator of a Territory; or

(ii) by a person authorised or empowered to do the act by an Australian law or a law of a foreign country—

is notified or published in the copy or document—

it is presumed, unless the contrary is proved, that the act was duly done and, if the day on which the act was done appears in the copy or document, it was done on that day.

Notes-2. See also section 143 of the Evidence (Miscellaneous Provisions) Act 1958 (Printing or using documents falsely purporting to be printed by government printer an indictable offence).

154. Documents published by authority of Parliaments etc.

It is presumed, unless the contrary is proved, that a document purporting to have been printed by authority of an Australian Parliament, a House of an Australian Parliament, a committee of such a House or a committee of an Australian Parliament—

(a) is what it purports to be; and

(b) was published on the day on which it purports to have been published.

155. Evidence of official records

(1) Evidence of a Commonwealth record or of a public document of this State, another State or a Territory may be adduced by producing a document that—

(a) purports to be such a record or document and to be signed or sealed by—

(i) a Minister of the Commonwealth, or a Minister of this or another State or a Territory, as the case requires; or

(ii) a person who might reasonably be supposed to have custody of the record or document; or

(b) purports to be a copy of or extract from the record or document that is certified to be a true copy or extract by—

(i) a Minister of the Commonwealth, or a Minister of this or another State or a Territory, as the case requires; or

(ii) a person who might reasonably be supposed to have custody of the record or document.

(2) If such a document is produced, it is presumed, unless evidence that is sufficient to raise doubt about the presumption is adduced, that—

(a) the document is the record, public document, copy or extract that it purports to be; and

(b) the Minister of the Commonwealth, Minister of this or that other State or the Territory or person—

(i) signed or sealed the record; or

(ii) certified the copy or extract as a true copy or extract—

as the case requires.

Note- The Commonwealth provision refers to evidence of a "public record" of a State or Territory rather than evidence of a "public document" of a State or Territory.

155A. Evidence of Commonwealth documents *****

.

156. Public documents

(1) A document that purports to be a copy of, or an extract from or summary of, a public document and to have been—

(a) sealed with the seal of a person who, or a body that, might reasonably be supposed to have the custody of the public document; or

(b) certified as such a copy, extract or summary by a person who might reasonably be supposed to have custody of the public document—

is presumed, unless the contrary is proved, to be a copy of the public document, or an extract from or summary of the public document.

(2) If an officer entrusted with the custody of a public document is required by a court to produce the public document, it is sufficient compliance with the requirement for the officer to produce a copy of, or extract from, the public document if it purports to be signed and certified by the officer as a true copy or extract.

(3) It is sufficient production of a copy or extract for the purposes of subsection (2) if the officer sends it by prepaid post, or causes it to be delivered, to—

(a) the proper officer of the court in which it is to be produced; or

(b) the person before whom it is to be produced.

(4) The court before which a copy or extract is produced under subsection (2) may direct the officer to produce the original public document.

157. Public documents relating to court processes

Evidence of a public document that is a judgment, act or other process of an Australian court or a foreign court, or that is a document lodged with an Australian court or a foreign court, may be adduced by producing a document that purports to be a copy of the public document and that—

(a) is proved to be an examined copy; or

(b) purports to be sealed with the seal of that court; or

(c) purports to be signed by a judge, magistrate, registrar or other proper officer of that court.

158. Evidence of certain public documents

(1) If—

(a) a public document, or a certified copy of a public document, of another State or a Territory is admissible for a purpose in that State or Territory under the law of that State or Territory; and

(b) it purports to be sealed, or signed and sealed, or signed alone, as directed by the law of that State or Territory—

it is admissible in evidence to the same extent and for that purpose in all Victorian courts—

(c) without proof of—

(i) the seal or signature; or

(ii) the official character of the person appearing to have signed it; and

(d) without further proof in every case in which the original document could have been received in evidence.

(2) A public document of another State or a Territory that is admissible in evidence for any purpose in that State or Territory under the law of that State or Territory without proof of—

(a) the seal or signature authenticating the document; or

(b) the judicial or official character of the person appearing to have signed the document—

is admissible in evidence to the same extent and for any purpose in all Victorian courts without such proof.

(3) This section only applies to documents that are public records of another State or a Territory.

159. Official statistics

A document that purports—

(a) to be published by the Australian Bureau of Statistics; and

(b) to contain statistics or abstracts compiled and analysed by the Australian Statistician under the Census and Statistics Act 1905 of the Commonwealth—

is evidence that those statistics or abstracts were compiled and analysed by the Australian Statistician under that Act.

Division 3—Matters relating to post and communications

160. Postal articles

(1) It is presumed (unless evidence sufficient to raise doubt about the presumption is adduced) that a postal article sent by prepaid post addressed to a person at a specified address in Australia or in an external Territory was received at that address on the seventh working day after having been posted.

(2) This section does not apply if—

(a) the proceeding relates to a contract; and

(b) all the parties to the proceeding are parties to the contract; and

(c) subsection (1) is inconsistent with a term of the contract.

(3) In this section, working day means a day that is not—

(a) a Saturday or a Sunday; or

(b) a public holiday or a bank holiday in the place to which the postal article was addressed.

161. Electronic communications

(1) If a document purports to contain a record of an electronic communication other than one referred to in section 162, it is presumed (unless evidence sufficient to raise doubt about the presumption is adduced) that the communication—

(a) was sent or made in the form of electronic communication that appears from the document to have been the form by which it was sent or made; and

(b) was sent or made by or on behalf of the person by or on whose behalf it appears from the document to have been sent or made; and

(c) was sent or made on the day on which, at the time at which and from the place from which it appears from the document to have been sent or made; and

(d) was received at the destination to which it appears from the document to have been sent; and

(e) if it appears from the document that the sending of the communication concluded at a particular time—was received at that destination at that time.

(2) A provision of subsection (1) does not apply if—

(a) the proceeding relates to a contract; and

(b) all the parties to the proceeding are parties to the contract; and

(c) the provision is inconsistent with a term of the contract.

162. Lettergrams and telegrams

(1) If a document purports to contain a record of a message transmitted by means of a lettergram or telegram, it is presumed (unless evidence sufficient to raise doubt about the presumption is adduced) that the message was received by the person to whom it was addressed 24 hours after the message was delivered to a post office for transmission as a lettergram or telegram.

(2) This section does not apply if—

(a) the proceeding relates to a contract; and

(b) all the parties to the proceeding are parties to the contract; and

(c) subsection (1) is inconsistent with a term of the contract.

163. Proof of letters having been sent by Commonwealth agencies *****

Part 4.4—Corroboration

164. Corroboration requirements abolished

(1) It is not necessary that evidence on which a party relies be corroborated.

(2) Subsection (1) does not affect the operation of a rule of law that requires corroboration with respect to the offence of perjury or a similar or related offence.

(3) Despite any rule, whether of law or practice, to the contrary, but subject to the other provisions of this Act, if there is a jury in a civil proceeding, it is not necessary that the judge—

    (a) warn the jury that it is dangerous to act on uncorroborated evidence or give a warning to the same or similar effect; or

    (b) give a direction relating to the absence of corroboration.

(4) Subject to subsection (5), if there is a jury in a criminal proceeding, the judge must not—

    (a) warn the jury that it is dangerous to act on uncorroborated evidence or give a warning to the same or similar effect; or

    (b) direct the jury regarding the absence of corroboration.

(5) In a criminal proceeding for the offence of perjury or a similar or related offence, the judge must direct the jury that it may find the accused guilty only if it is satisfied that the evidence proving guilt is corroborated.

(6) The principles and rules of the common law that relate to jury directions or warnings on corroboration of evidence, or the absence of corroboration of evidence, in criminal trials to the contrary of this section are abolished.

Part 4.5—Warnings and information
165. Unreliable evidence

(1) This section applies to evidence in a civil proceeding that is evidence of a kind that may be unreliable, including the following kinds of evidence—

(a) evidence in relation to which Part 3.2 (hearsay evidence) or 3.4 (admissions) applies;

(b) identification evidence;

(c) evidence the reliability of which may be affected by age, ill health (whether physical or mental), injury or the like;

*****

(g) in a proceeding against the estate of a deceased person—evidence adduced by or on behalf of a person seeking relief in the proceeding that is evidence about a matter about which the deceased person could have given evidence if he or she were alive.

(2) If there is a jury and a party so requests, the judge is to—

(a) warn the jury that the evidence may be unreliable; and

(b) inform the jury of matters that may cause it to be unreliable; and

(c) warn the jury of the need for caution in determining whether to accept the evidence and the weight to be given to it.

(3) The judge need not comply with subsection (2) if there are good reasons for not doing so.

(4) It is not necessary that a particular form of words be used in giving the warning or information.

(5) This section does not affect any other power of the judge to give a warning to, or to inform, the jury.

(6) Subsection (2) does not permit a judge to warn or inform a jury in proceedings before it in which a child gives evidence that the reliability of the child's evidence may be affected by the age of the child. Any such warning or information may be given only in accordance with section 165A(2) and (3).

> **Note -** This section applies only to civil proceedings. Divisions 3 and 4 of Part 4 of the Jury Directions Act 2015 contain provisions relating to unreliable evidence and identification evidence that apply in criminal trials.

165A. Warnings in relation to children's evidence

(1) A judge in any civil proceeding in which evidence is given by a child before a jury must not do any of the following—

(a) warn the jury, or suggest to the jury, that children as a class are unreliable witnesses;

(b) warn the jury, or suggest to the jury, that the evidence of children as a class is inherently less credible or reliable, or requires more careful scrutiny, than the evidence of adults;

(c) give a warning, or suggestion to the jury, about the unreliability of the particular child's evidence solely on account of the age of the child.

*****

(2) Subsection (1) does not prevent the judge, at the request of a party, from—

(a) informing the jury that the evidence of the particular child may be unreliable and the reasons why it may be unreliable; and

(b) warning or informing the jury of the need for caution in determining whether to accept the evidence of the particular child and the weight to be given to it—

if the party has satisfied the court that there are circumstances (other than solely the age of the child) particular to the child that affect the reliability of the child's evidence and that warrant the giving of a warning or the information.

(3) This section does not affect any other power of a judge to give a warning to, or to inform, the jury.

> **Note** - This section applies only to civil proceedings. Division 3 of Part 4 of the Jury Directions Act 2015 contains provisions relating to children's evidence that apply in criminal trials.

165B. Delay in prosecution *****

Note- Division 5 of Part 4 of the Jury Directions Act 2015 contains provisions relating to delay and forensic disadvantage that apply in criminal trials.

Part 4.6—Ancillary provisions
Division 1—Requests to produce documents
or call witnesses

166. Definition of request
In this Division, **request** means a request that a party (the requesting party) makes to another party to do one or more of the following—

(a) to produce to the requesting party the whole or a part of a specified document or thing;

(b) to permit the requesting party, adequately and in an appropriate way, to examine, test or copy the whole or a part of a specified document or thing;

(c) to call as a witness a specified person believed to be concerned in the production or maintenance of a specified document or thing;

(d) to call as a witness a specified person in whose possession or under whose control a specified document or thing is believed to be or to have been at any time;

(e) in relation to a document of the kind referred to in paragraph (b) or (c) of the definition of document in the Dictionary—to permit the requesting party, adequately and in an appropriate way, to examine and test the document and the way in which it was produced and has been kept;

(f) in relation to evidence of a previous representation—to call as a witness the person who made the previous representation;

(g) in relation to evidence that a person has been convicted of an offence, being evidence to which section 92(2) applies—to call as a witness a person who gave evidence in the proceeding in which the person was so convicted.

167. Requests may be made about certain matters
A party may make a reasonable request to another party for the purpose of determining a question that relates to—

(a) a previous representation; or

(b) evidence of a conviction of a person for an offence; or

(c) the authenticity, identity or admissibility of a document or thing.

168. Time limits for making certain requests
(1) If a party has given to another party written notice of its intention to adduce evidence of a previous representation, the other party may only make a request to the party relating to the representation if the request is made within 21 days after the notice was given.

(2) Despite subsection (1), the court may give the other party leave to make a request relating to the representation after the end of that 21 day period if it is satisfied that there is a good reason to do so.

(3) If a party has given to another party written notice of its intention to adduce evidence of a person's conviction of an offence in order to prove a fact in issue, the other party may only make a request relating to evidence of the conviction if the request is made within 21 days after the notice is given.

(4) Despite subsection (3), the court may give the other party leave to make a request relating to evidence of the conviction after the end of that 21 day period if it is satisfied that there is good reason to do so.

(5) If a party has served on another party a copy of a document that it intends to tender in evidence, the other party may only make a request relating to the document if the request is made within 21 days after service of the copy.

(6) If the copy of the document served under subsection (5) is accompanied by, or has endorsed on it, a notice stating that the document is to be tendered to prove the contents of another document, the other party may only make a request relating to the other document if the request is made within 21 days after service of the copy.

(7) Despite subsections (5) and (6), the court may give the other party leave to make a request relating to the document, or other document, after the end of the 21 day period if it is satisfied that there is good reason to do so.

169. Failure or refusal to comply with requests

(1) If the party has, without reasonable cause, failed or refused to comply with a request, the court may, on application, make one or more of the following orders—

(a) an order directing the party to comply with the request;

(b) an order that the party produce a specified document or thing, or call as a witness a specified person, as mentioned in section 166;

(c) an order that the evidence in relation to which the request was made is not to be admitted in evidence;

(d) such order with respect to adjournment or costs as is just.

(2) If the party had, within a reasonable time after receiving the request, informed the other party that it refuses to comply with the request, any application under subsection (1) by the other party must be made within a reasonable time after being so informed.

(3) The court may, on application, direct that evidence in relation to which a request was made is not to be admitted in evidence if an order made by it under subsection (1)(a) or (b) is not complied with.

(4) Without limiting the circumstances that may constitute reasonable cause for a party to fail to comply with a request, it is reasonable cause to fail to comply with a request if—

(a) the document or thing to be produced is not available to the party; or

(b) the existence and contents of the document are not in issue in the proceeding in which evidence of the document is proposed to be adduced; or

(c) the person to be called as a witness is not available.

(5) Without limiting the matters that the court may take into account in relation to the exercise of a power under subsection (1), it is to take into account—

(a) the importance in the proceeding of the evidence in relation to which the request was made; and

(b) whether there is likely to be a dispute about the matter to which the evidence relates; and

(c) whether there is a reasonable doubt as to the authenticity or accuracy of the evidence that is, or the document the contents of which are, sought to be proved; and

(d) whether there is a reasonable doubt as to the authenticity of the document or thing that is sought to be tendered; and

(e) if the request relates to evidence of a previous representation—whether there is a reasonable doubt as to the accuracy of the representation or of the evidence on which it was based; and

(f) in the case of a request referred to in paragraph (g) of the definition of request in section 166—whether another person is available to give evidence about the conviction or the facts that were in issue in the proceeding in which the conviction was obtained; and

(g) whether compliance with the request would involve undue expense or delay or would not be reasonably practicable; and

(h) the nature of the proceeding.

Note-Clause 5 of Part 2 of the Dictionary is about the availability of documents and things, and clause 4 of Part 2 of the Dictionary is about the availability of persons.

Division 2—Proof of certain matters by affidavits or written statements

170. Evidence relating to certain matters

(1) Evidence of a fact that is, because of a provision of this Act referred to in the Table, to be proved in relation to a document or thing may be given by a person permitted under section 171 to give such evidence.

Table

Provisions of this Act	Subject-matter
Section 48	Proof of contents of documents
Sections 63, 64 and 65	Hearsay exceptions for "first-hand" hearsay
Section 69	Hearsay exception for business records
Section 70	Hearsay exception for tags, labels and other writing
Section 71	Hearsay exception for telecommunications
The provisions of Part 4.3	Facilitation of proof

Note-The Table to section 170 of the Commonwealth Act includes a reference to section 182 (Commonwealth records) of that Act.

(2) Evidence may be given by affidavit or, if the evidence relates to a public document, by a written statement.

171. Persons who may give such evidence
(1) Such evidence may be given by—
    (a) a person who, at the relevant time or afterwards, had a position of responsibility in relation to making or keeping the document or thing; or
    (b) except in the case of evidence of a fact that is to be proved in relation to a document or thing because of section 63, 64 or 65—an authorised person.
(2) Despite subsection (1)(b), evidence must not be given under this section by an authorised person who, at the relevant time or afterwards, did not have a position of responsibility in relation to making or keeping the document or thing unless it appears to the court that—
    (a) it is not reasonably practicable for the evidence to be given by a person who had, at the relevant time or afterwards, a position of responsibility in relation to making or keeping the document or thing; or
    (b) having regard to all the circumstances of the case, undue expense would be caused by calling such a person as a witness.
(3) In this section, authorised person means—
    (a) a person before whom an affidavit may be sworn and taken in a country or place outside the State under section 21 of the Oaths and Affirmations Act 2018; or
    (b) a member of the police force above the rank of sergeant; or
    (c) a person authorised by the Attorney-General for the purposes of this section.

172. Evidence based on knowledge, belief or information
(1) Despite Chapter 3, the evidence may include evidence based on the knowledge and belief of the person who gives it, or on information that that person has.
(2) An affidavit or statement that includes evidence based on knowledge, information or belief must set out the source of the knowledge or information or the basis of the belief.

173. Notification of other parties
(1) A copy of the affidavit or statement must be served on each party a reasonable time before the hearing of the proceeding.
(2) The party who tenders the affidavit or statement must, if another party so requests, call the deponent or person who made the statement to give evidence but need not otherwise do so.

Division 3—Foreign law

174. Evidence of foreign law

(1) Evidence of a statute, proclamation, treaty or act of state of a foreign country may be adduced in a proceeding by producing—

(a) a book or pamphlet, containing the statute, proclamation, treaty or act of state, that purports to have been printed by the government or official printer of the country or by the authority of the government or administration of the country; or

(b) a book or other publication, containing the statute, proclamation, treaty or act of state, that appears to the court to be a reliable source of information; or

(c) a book or pamphlet that is or would be used in the courts of the country to inform the courts about, or prove, the statute, proclamation, treaty or act of state; or

(d) a copy of the statute, proclamation, treaty or act of state that is proved to be an examined copy.

(2) A reference in this section to a statute of a foreign country includes a reference to a regulation or by-law of the country.

175. Evidence of law reports of foreign countries

(1) Evidence of the unwritten or common law of a foreign country may be adduced by producing a book containing reports of judgments of courts of the country if the book is or would be used in the courts of the country to inform the courts about the unwritten or common law of the country.

(2) Evidence of the interpretation of a statute of a foreign country may be adduced by producing a book containing reports of judgments of courts of the country if the book is or would be used in the courts of the country to inform the courts about the interpretation of the statute.

176. Questions of foreign law to be decided by judge

If, in a proceeding in which there is a jury, it is necessary to ascertain the law of another country which is applicable to the facts of the case, any question as to the effect of the evidence adduced with respect to that law is to be decided by the judge alone.

Division 4—Procedures for proving other matters

177. Certificates of expert evidence

(1) Evidence of a person's opinion may be adduced by tendering a certificate (expert certificate) signed by the person that—

(a) states the person's name and address; and

(b) states that the person has specialised knowledge based on his or her training, study or experience as specified in the certificate; and

(c) sets out an opinion that the person holds and that is expressed to be wholly or substantially based on that knowledge.

(2) Subsection (1) does not apply unless the party seeking to tender the expert certificate has served on each other party—

(a) a copy of the certificate; and

(b) a written notice stating that the party proposes to tender the certificate as evidence of the opinion.

(3) Service must be effected not later than—

(a) 21 days before the hearing; or

(b) if, on application by the party before or after service, the court substitutes a different period—the beginning of that period.

(4) Service for the purposes of subsection (2) may be proved by affidavit.

(5) A party on whom the documents referred to in subsection (2) are served may, by written notice served on the party proposing to tender the expert certificate, require the party to call the person who signed the certificate to give evidence.

(6) The expert certificate is not admissible as evidence if such a requirement is made.

(7) The court may make such order with respect to costs as it considers just against a party who has, without reasonable cause, required a party to call a person to give evidence under this section.

178. Convictions, acquittals and other judicial proceedings

(1) This section applies to the following facts—
(a) the conviction or acquittal before or by an applicable court of a person charged with an offence;
(b) the sentencing of a person to any punishment or pecuniary penalty by an applicable court;
(c) an order by an applicable court;
(d) the pendency or existence at any time before an applicable court of a civil or criminal proceeding.

(2) Evidence of a fact to which this section applies may be given by a certificate signed by a judge, a magistrate or registrar or other proper officer of the applicable court—
(a) showing the fact, or purporting to contain particulars, of the record, indictment, conviction, acquittal, sentence, order or proceeding in question; and
(b) stating the time and place of the conviction, acquittal, sentence, order or proceeding; and
(c) stating the title of the applicable court.

(3) A certificate given under this section showing a conviction, acquittal, sentence or order is also evidence of the particular offence or matter in respect of which the conviction, acquittal, sentence or order was had, passed or made, if stated in the certificate.

(4) A certificate given under this section showing the pendency or existence of a proceeding is also evidence of the particular nature and occasion, or ground and cause, of the proceeding, if stated in the certificate.

(5) A certificate given under this section purporting to contain particulars of a record, indictment, conviction, acquittal, sentence, order or proceeding is also evidence of the matters stated in the certificate.

(6) In this section—
acquittal includes the dismissal of the charge in question by an applicable court;
applicable court means an Australian court or a foreign court.

> **Note**-Section 91 excludes evidence of certain judgments and convictions.

179. Proof of identity of convicted persons—affidavits by members of State or Territory police forces

(1) This section applies if a member of a police force of a State or Territory—

(a) makes an affidavit in the form prescribed by the regulations for the purposes of this section; and

(b) states in the affidavit that he or she is a fingerprint expert for that police force.

(2) For the purpose of proving before a court the identity of a person alleged to have been convicted in that State or Territory of an offence, the affidavit is evidence in a proceeding that the person whose fingerprints are shown on a fingerprint card referred to in the affidavit and marked for identification—

(a) is the person referred to in a certificate of conviction, or certified copy of conviction annexed to the affidavit, as having been convicted of an offence; and

(b) was convicted of that offence; and

(c) was convicted of any other offence of which he or she is stated in the affidavit to have been convicted.

(3) For the purposes of this section, if a Territory does not have its own police force, the police force performing the policing functions of the Territory is taken to be the police force of the Territory.

180. Proof of identity of convicted persons—affidavits by members of Australian Federal Police

(1) This section applies if a member of the Australian Federal Police—

(a) makes an affidavit in the form prescribed by the regulations for the purposes of this section; and

(b) states in the affidavit that he or she is a fingerprint expert for the Australian Federal Police.

(2) For the purpose of proving before a court the identity of a person alleged to have been convicted of an offence against a law of the Commonwealth, the affidavit is evidence in a proceeding that the person whose fingerprints are shown on a fingerprint card referred to in the affidavit and marked for identification—

(a) is the person referred to in a certificate of conviction, or certified copy of conviction annexed to the affidavit, as having been convicted of an offence; and

(b) was convicted of that offence; and

(c) was convicted of any other offence of which he or she is stated in the affidavit to have been convicted.

181. Proof of service of statutory notifications, notices, orders and directions

(1) The service, giving or sending under an Australian law of a written notification, notice, order or direction may be proved by affidavit of the person who served, gave or sent it.

(2) A person who, for the purposes of a proceeding, makes an affidavit referred to in this section is not, because of making the affidavit, excused from attending for cross-examination if required to do so by a party to the proceeding.

Chapter 5—Miscellaneous

182. Application of certain sections in relation to Commonwealth records
*****

183. Inferences
If a question arises about the application of a provision of this Act in relation to a document or thing, the court may—
(a) examine the document or thing; and
(b) draw any reasonable inferences from it as well as from other matters from which inferences may properly be drawn.

184. Accused may admit matters and give consents
(1) In or before a criminal proceeding, an accused may—
(a) admit matters of fact; and
(b) give any consent—
that a party to a civil proceeding may make or give.
(2) An admission made by or a consent given by an accused is not effective for the purposes of subsection (1) unless—
(a) the accused has been advised to do so by the Australian legal practitioner of the accused; or
(b) the court is satisfied that the accused understands the consequences of making the admission or giving the consent.

185. Full faith and credit to be given to documents properly authenticated
*****

186. Swearing or affirming of affidavits
***** **Notes-** 1. Part 3 of the Oaths and Affirmations Act 2018 relates to affidavits.

187. No privilege against self-incrimination for bodies corporate
(1) This section applies if, under a law of the State or in a proceeding, a body corporate is required to—
(a) answer a question or give information; or
(b) produce a document or any other thing; or
(c) do any other act whatever.
(2) The body corporate is not entitled to refuse or fail to comply with the requirement on the ground that answering the question, giving the information, producing the document or other thing or doing that other act, as the case may be, might tend to incriminate the body or make the body liable to a penalty.

188. Impounding documents
The court may direct that a document that has been tendered or produced before the court (whether or not it is admitted in evidence) is to be impounded and kept in the custody of an officer of the court or of another person for such period, and subject to such conditions, as the court thinks fit.

189. The voir dire

(1) If the determination of a question whether—

(a) evidence should be admitted (whether in the exercise of a discretion or not); or

(b) evidence can be used against a person; or

(c) a witness is competent or compellable—

depends on the court finding that a particular fact exists, the question whether that fact exists is, for the purposes of this section, a preliminary question.

(2) If there is a jury, a preliminary question whether—

(a) particular evidence is evidence of an admission, or evidence to which section 138 (Discretion to exclude improperly or illegally obtained evidence) applies; or

(b) evidence of an admission, or evidence to which section 138 applies, should be admitted—

is to be heard and determined in the jury's absence.

(3) In the hearing of a preliminary question about whether an admission made by an accused should be admitted into evidence (whether in the exercise of a discretion or not) in a criminal proceeding, the issue of the admission's truth or untruth is to be disregarded unless the issue is introduced by the accused.

(4) If there is a jury, the jury is not to be present at a hearing to decide any other preliminary question unless the court so orders.

(5) Without limiting the matters that the court may take into account in deciding whether to make such an order, it is to take into account—

(a) whether the evidence to be adduced in the course of that hearing is likely to be prejudicial to the accused; and

(b) whether the evidence concerned will be adduced in the course of the hearing to decide the preliminary question; and

(c) whether the evidence to be adduced in the course of that hearing would be admitted if adduced at another stage of the hearing (other than in another hearing to decide a preliminary question or, in a criminal proceeding, a hearing in relation to sentencing).

(6) Section 128(10) does not apply to a hearing to decide a preliminary question.

(7) In the application of Chapter 3 to a hearing to determine a preliminary question, the facts in issue are taken to include the fact to which the hearing relates.

(8) If a jury in a proceeding was not present at a hearing to determine a preliminary question, evidence is not to be adduced in the proceeding of evidence given by a witness at the hearing unless—

(a) it is inconsistent with other evidence given by the witness in the proceeding; or

(b) the witness has died.

190. Waiver of rules of evidence

(1) The court may, if the parties consent, by order dispense with the application of any one or more of the provisions of—

(a) Division 3, 4 or 5 of Part 2.1; or

(b) Part 2.2 or 2.3; or

(c) Parts 3.2–3.8—

in relation to particular evidence or generally.

(2) In a criminal proceeding, a consent given by an accused is not effective for the purposes of subsection (1) unless—

(a) the accused has been advised to do so by the Australian legal practitioner of the accused; or

(b) the court is satisfied that the accused understands the consequences of giving the consent.

(3) In a civil proceeding, the court may order that any one or more of the provisions mentioned in subsection (1) do not apply in relation to evidence if—

(a) the matter to which the evidence relates is not genuinely in dispute; or

(b) the application of those provisions would cause or involve unnecessary expense or delay.

(4) Without limiting the matters that the court may take into account in deciding whether to exercise the power conferred by subsection (3), it is to take into account—

(a) the importance of the evidence in the proceeding; and

(b) the nature of the cause of action or defence and the nature of the subject-matter of the proceeding; and

(c) the probative value of the evidence; and

(d) the powers of the court (if any) to adjourn the hearing, to make another order or to give a direction in relation to the evidence.

191. Agreements as to facts

(1) In this section, agreed fact means a fact that the parties to a proceeding have agreed is not, for the purposes of the proceeding, to be disputed.

(2) In a proceeding—

(a) evidence is not required to prove the existence of an agreed fact; and

(b) evidence may not be adduced to contradict or qualify an agreed fact—

unless the court gives leave.

(3) Subsection (2) does not apply unless the agreed fact—

(a) is stated in an agreement in writing signed by the parties or by Australian legal practitioners or prosecutors representing the parties and adduced in evidence in the proceeding; or

(b) with the leave of the court, is stated by a party before the court with the agreement of all other parties.

192. Leave, permission or direction may be given on terms

(1) If, because of this Act, a court may give any leave, permission or direction, the leave, permission or direction may be given on such terms as the court thinks fit.

(2) Without limiting the matters that the court may take into account in deciding whether to give the leave, permission or direction, it is to take into account—

(a) the extent to which to do so would be likely to add unduly to, or to shorten, the length of the hearing; and

(b) the extent to which to do so would be unfair to a party or to a witness; and

(c) the importance of the evidence in relation to which the leave, permission or direction is sought; and

(d) the nature of the proceeding; and

(e) the power (if any) of the court to adjourn the hearing or to make another order or to give a direction in relation to the evidence.

192A. Advance rulings and findings

Where a question arises in any proceedings, being a question about—

(a) the admissibility or use of evidence proposed to be adduced; or

(b) the operation of a provision of this Act or another law in relation to evidence proposed to be adduced; or

(c) the giving of leave, permission or direction under section 192—

the court may, if it considers it to be appropriate to do so, give a ruling or make a finding in relation to the question before the evidence is adduced in the proceedings.

193. Additional powers

(1) The powers of a court in relation to—

(a) the discovery or inspection of documents; and

(b) ordering disclosure and exchange of evidence, intended evidence, documents and reports—

extend to enabling the court to make such orders as the court thinks fit (including orders about methods of inspection, adjournments and costs) to ensure that the parties to a proceeding can adequately, and in an appropriate manner, inspect documents of the kind referred to in paragraph (b) or (c) of the definition of document in the Dictionary.

(2) The power of a person or body to make rules of courts extends to making rules, not inconsistent with this Act or the regulations, prescribing matters—

(a) required or permitted by this Act to be prescribed; or

(b) necessary or convenient to be prescribed for carrying out or giving effect to this Act.

(3) Without limiting subsection (2), rules made under that subsection may provide for the discovery, exchange, inspection or disclosure of intended evidence, documents and reports of persons intended to be called by a party to give evidence in a proceeding.

(4) Without limiting subsection (2), rules made under that subsection may provide for the exclusion of evidence, or for its admission on specified terms, if the rules are not complied with.

194.Witnesses failing to attend proceedings

(1) If, in a civil or criminal proceeding, a witness fails to appear when called and it is proved that the witness has been—

(a) bound over to appear; or

(b) duly bound by recognisance or undertaking to appear; or

(c) served with a summons or subpoena to attend and a reasonable sum of money has been provided to the witness for his or her costs in so attending—

the court may—

(d) issue a warrant to apprehend the witness and bring him or her before the court; or

(e) order the witness to pay a fine of not more than 5 penalty units; or

(f) take any other action against the witness that is permitted by law.

(2) If a subpoena or summons has been issued for the attendance of a witness on the hearing of a civil or criminal proceeding and it is proved, on application by the party seeking to compel his or her attendance, that the witness—

(a) is avoiding service of the subpoena or summons; or

(b) has been duly served with the subpoena or summons but is unlikely to comply with it—

the court may issue a warrant to apprehend the witness and bring the witness before the court.

(3) In issuing a warrant under this section, the court may endorse the warrant with a direction that the person must, on arrest, be released on bail as specified in the endorsement.

(4) An endorsement under subsection (3) must fix the amounts in which the principal and the sureties (if any) are bound and the amount of any money or the value of any security to be deposited.

(5) The person to whom the warrant to arrest is directed must cause the person named or described in the warrant when arrested—

(a) to be released on bail in accordance with any endorsement on the warrant; or

(b) if there is no endorsement on the warrant, to be brought before the court which issued the warrant; or

(c) to be discharged from custody on bail in accordance with the Bail Act 1977.

(6) Matters may be proved under this section orally or by affidavit.

(7) A witness, who under subsection (1)(e) has been ordered to pay a fine, is not exempted from any other proceedings for disobeying the subpoena or summons.

195. Prohibited question not to be published

A person must not, without the express permission of a court, print or publish—

(a) any question that the court has disallowed under section 41 (Improper questions); or

(b) any question that the court has disallowed because any answer that is likely to be given to the question would contravene the credibility rule; or

(c) any question in respect of which the court has refused to give leave under Part 3.7 (Credibility).

Penalty: 60 penalty units.

196. Proceedings for offences
■■

197. Regulations
(1) The Governor in Council may make regulations for or with respect to any matter or thing that is required or permitted to be prescribed or necessary to be prescribed to give effect to this Act.
(2) The regulations—
    (a) may be of general or limited application; and
    (b) may differ according to differences in time, place or circumstance.

Schedule 1—Oaths and affirmations
Oaths by witnesses
I swear (or the person taking the oath may promise) by Almighty God (or the person may name a god recognised by his or her religion) that the evidence I shall give will be the truth, the whole truth and nothing but the truth.

Oaths by interpreters
I swear (or the person taking the oath may promise) by Almighty God (or the person may name a god recognised by his or her religion) that I will well and truly interpret the evidence that will be given and do all other matters and things that are required of me in this case to the best of my ability.

Affirmations by witnesses
I solemnly and sincerely declare and affirm that the evidence I shall give will be the truth, the whole truth and nothing but the truth.

Affirmations by interpreters
I solemnly and sincerely declare and affirm that I will well and truly interpret the evidence that will be given and do all other matters and things that are required of me in this case to the best of my ability.

Schedule 2—Transitional provisions
Part 1—General
1. Definitions
In this Schedule—
commencement day means the day this Act (other than Part 1 and the Dictionary) commences.

2. Application of this Act on commencement day
(1) Except as otherwise provided by this Schedule, this Act applies to any proceeding (within the operation of section 4) commenced on or after the commencement day.
(2) Except as otherwise provided by this Schedule, in the case of any proceeding (within the operation of section 4) that commenced before the commencement day, this Act applies to that part of the proceeding that takes place on or after the commencement day, other than any hearing in the proceeding that commenced before the commencement day and—
    (a) continued on or after the commencement day; or
    (b) was adjourned until the commencement day or a day after the commencement day.

3. Application of section 128A

Section 128A does not apply to an order made before the commencement day that would, if it were made after the commencement day, be a disclosure order within the meaning of that section.

4. Application of Part 3.10 to disclosure requirements

(1) Part 3.10 does not apply in respect of—

(a) a process or order of the court that requires the disclosure of information or a document issued or ordered before the commencement day that would, if it were issued or ordered after the commencement day, be a disclosure requirement within the meaning of section 131A; or

(b) a summons or subpoena issued on or after the commencement day to give evidence or produce documents at a hearing to which clause 2(2)(a) or (b) applies.

(2) Despite subclause (1)(a), Part 3.10 applies to a summons or subpoena to give evidence issued before the commencement day if the evidence is to be given at a hearing to which this Act applies.

5. Identifications already carried out

(1) Section 114 does not apply in relation to an identification made before the commencement day.

(2) Section 115 does not apply in relation to an identification made before the commencement day.

6. Documents and evidence produced before commencement day by processes, machines and other devices

(1) Section 146 has effect on and from the commencement day with respect to the production of a document or thing that occurred before the commencement day.

(2) Section 147 has effect on and from the commencement day with respect to the production of a document that occurred before the commencement day.

7. Documents attested and verified before the commencement day

(1) Section 148 has effect on and from the commencement day with respect to the attestation, verification, signing or acknowledgement of a document that occurred before the commencement day.

(2) Section 149 has effect on and from the commencement day with respect to the attestation or signing of a document that occurred before the commencement day.

8. Matters of official record published before the commencement day

(1) Section 153 has effect on and from the commencement day with respect to the publication of a document referred to in that section that occurred before the commencement day.

(2) Section 154 has effect on and from the commencement day with respect to the publication of a document referred to in that section that occurred before the commencement day.

(3) Section 155 has effect on and from the commencement day with respect to the signing and sealing or certification of a document referred to in that section that occurred before the commencement day.

(4) Section 156 has effect on and from the commencement day with respect to the sealing or certification of a document referred to in that section that occurred before the commencement day.

(5) Section 157 has effect on and from the commencement day with respect to the sealing or signing of a document referred to in that section that occurred before the commencement day.

(6) Section 158 has effect on and from the commencement day with respect to the sealing or signing and sealing of a public document referred to in that section that occurred before the commencement day.

(7) Section 159 has effect on and from the commencement day with respect to the publication of a document referred to in that section that occurred before the commencement day.

9. Agreed facts

The reference in section 191(3)(a) to an agreement is taken on and from the commencement day to include a reference to an agreement entered into before the commencement day under section 149AB(3) of the Evidence Act 1958, as in force immediately before its repeal.

10. Application of Act to improperly or illegally obtained evidence

Section 139 does not apply in relation to a statement made or an act done before the commencement day.

Part 2—Application of notification provisions

11. Notification provisions

(1) If, before the commencement day, a document of a kind referred to in a notification provision is given or served—

    (a) in the circumstances provided for in that provision; and

    (b) in accordance with such requirements (if any) as would apply to the giving or serving of the document under that provision on and after its commencement—

on and from the commencement day the document is taken to have been given or served in accordance with that provision.

(2) The following sections are notification provisions for the purposes of subclause (1)—

    (a) section 33(2)(c);

    (b) section 49(a);

    (c) section 50(2)(a);

    (d) section 67(1);

    (e) section 68(2);

    (f) section 73(2)(b);

    (g) section 97;

    (h) section 98;

    (i) sections 168(1), (3), (5) and (6);

    (j) section 173(1);

    (k) sections 177(2) and 177(5).

12. Notice of intention to adduce hearsay evidence

If a notice given before the commencement day is taken, by the operation of clause 11, to have been given under section 67(1), the period for an objection to be made under section 68 to the tender of evidence to which the notice relates is the later of the period ending—

    (a) 7 days after the commencement day; or

    (b) 21 days after the notice was given to the party concerned.

13. Notice of intention to adduce evidence as to tendency or coincidence

(1) References in sections 97(1)(a) and 98(1)(a) to giving notice are taken to include references to giving notice of the kind referred to in those sections before the commencement day.

(2) Despite clause 11(1)(b), a notice of a kind referred to in section 97 or 98 given before the commencement day is taken to have been given in accordance with any regulations or rules made for the purposes for section 99.

14. Time limits for making requests

(1) A request made before the commencement day that would, if it were made after the commencement day be a request under section 167, is taken to be such a request.

(2) If a notice given before the commencement day is taken, by the operation of clause 11, to have been given under section 168(1) or (3), the period for a request to be made under section 168(1) or (3) is the later of the period ending—

    (a) 7 days after the commencement day; or

    (b) 21 days after the notice was given to the party concerned.

(3) If a copy of a document served before the commencement day is taken, by the operation of clause 11, to have been served under section 168(5) or (6), the period for a request to be made under section 168(5) or (6) is the later of the period ending—

    (a) 7 days after the commencement day; or

    (b) 21 days after the document was served on the party concerned.

(4) If a request made under section 168 was received before the commencement day, in determining what is a reasonable time after receiving a request for the purposes of section 169(2), the court may take into account time passed before the commencement day.

15. Requests under section 173

A request made before the commencement day that would, if it were made after the commencement day be a request under section 173(2), is taken to be such a request.

16. Proof of voluminous or complex documents

If a court has given a direction under section 42B of the Evidence Act 1958, as in force immediately before its repeal, and a party has been provided with a copy of the evidence in the form specified in that direction, the party is taken, for the purposes of section 50(2)(b), to have been given a reasonable opportunity to examine or copy documents.

Part 3—Transitional provisions for Evidence Amendment (Journalist Privilege) Act 2012

17. Definitions

In this Part—

2012 Act means the Evidence Amendment (Journalist Privilege) Act 2012.

18. Application of Division 1C of Part 3.10

(1) Except as otherwise provided by this Schedule, the amendment made to Part 3.10 of this Act by section 3 of the 2012 Act applies to any proceeding commenced on or after the commencement of that section.

(2) Except as otherwise provided by this Schedule, in the case of any proceeding that commenced before the commencement of section 3 of the 2012 Act, the amendment made to Part 3.10 of this Act by that section applies to that part of the proceeding that takes place on or after the commencement of that section, other than any hearing in the proceeding that commenced before the commencement of that section and—

    (a) continued on or after the commencement of that section; or

    (b) was adjourned until the commencement of that section or a day after the commencement of that section.

19. Application of Division 1C of Part 3.10 to disclosure requirements

(1) The amendment made to Part 3.10 of this Act by section 3 of the 2012 Act does not apply in respect of—

(a) a disclosure requirement issued or ordered before the commencement of section 3 of that Act; or

(b) a disclosure requirement issued or ordered on or after the commencement of section 3 of that Act to give evidence or produce documents at a hearing to which clause 18(2)(a) or (b) applies.

(2) Despite subclause (1)(a), the amendment made to Part 3.10 of this Act by section 3 of the 2012 Act applies to a disclosure requirement issued or ordered before the commencement of section 3 of that Act if the evidence is to be given at a hearing to which the amendment made by section 3 of that Act applies.

(3) In this section, disclosure requirement has the same meaning as in section 131A.

20. Certificate given to a witness before commencement

(1) The amendment made to section 128 by section 4(3) and (4) of the 2012 Act has effect on and from the commencement of that section with respect to the giving of a certificate under a prescribed State or Territory provision that has occurred before the commencement of that section.

(2) The amendment made to section 128A by section 5 of the 2012 Act has effect on and from the commencement of that section with respect to the giving of a certificate under a prescribed State or Territory provision that has occurred before the commencement of that section.

Part 5—Transitional provision for Crimes Amendment (Abolition of Defensive Homicide) Act 2014

22. Transitional—Crimes Amendment (Abolition of Defensive Homicide) Act 2014

This Act as amended by Part 3 of the Crimes Amendment (Abolition of Defensive Homicide) Act 2014 applies to a trial that commences (within the meaning of section 210 of the Criminal Procedure Act 2009) on or after the day on which Part 3 of the Crimes Amendment (Abolition of Defensive Homicide) Act 2014 comes into operation, irrespective of when the offence is alleged to have been committed.

23. Application of Act as amended

This Act as amended by Division 2 of Part 10 of the Jury Directions Act 2015 applies to a trial that commences (within the meaning of section 210 of the Criminal Procedure Act 2009) on or after the day on which Division 2 of Part 10 of that Act comes into operation.

Part 7—Transitional provision for Jury Directions and Other Acts Amendment Act 2017

24. Application of section 66 as amended

Section 66 as amended by section 17 of the Jury Directions and Other Acts Amendment Act 2017 applies to—

(a) a trial that commences (within the meaning of section 210 of the Criminal Procedure Act 2009) on or after the day on which section 17 of the Jury Directions and Other Acts Amendment Act 2017 comes into operation; and

(b) a summary hearing held on or after the day on which section 17 of the Jury Directions and Other Acts Amendment Act 2017 comes into operation if no evidence has been given in that hearing before that day.

Dictionary
Part 1—Definitions

ACT court
Note - The Commonwealth Act includes a definition of this term.
admission means a previous representation that is—

(a) made by a person who is or becomes a party to a proceeding (including an accused in a criminal proceeding); and

(b) adverse to the person's interest in the outcome of the proceeding;
asserted fact is defined in section 59;
associated accused, in relation to an accused in a criminal proceeding, means a person against whom a prosecution has been instituted, but not yet completed or terminated, for—

(a) an offence that arose in relation to the same events as those in relation to which the offence for which the accused is being prosecuted arose; or

(b) an offence that relates to or is connected with the offence for which the accused is being prosecuted;
Australia includes the external Territories;
Australian court means—

(a) the High Court; or

(b) a court **exercising** federal jurisdiction; or

(c) a court of a State or Territory; or

(d) a judge, justice or arbitrator under an Australian law; or

(e) a person or body authorised by an Australian law, or by consent of parties, to hear, receive and examine evidence; or

(f) a person or body that, in exercising a function under an Australian law, is required to apply the laws of evidence;
Australian law means a law of the Commonwealth, a State or a Territory;
  Note-See clause 9 of Part 2 of this Dictionary for the meaning of law.
Australian or overseas proceeding means a proceeding (however described) in an Australian court or a foreign court;

Australian Parliament means the Parliament, the Parliament of the
Commonwealth or another State or the Legislative Assembly of a Territory;

Australian-registered foreign lawyer has the meaning it has in the Legal
Profession Uniform Law (Victoria);

Australian Statistician means the Australian Statistician referred to in section
5(2) of the Australian Bureau of Statistics Act 1975 of the Commonwealth,
and includes any person to whom the powers of the Australian Statistician
under section 12 of the Census and Statistics Act 1905 of the
Commonwealth have been delegated;

business is defined in clause 1 of Part 2 of this Dictionary;

case of a party means the facts in issue in respect of which the party bears the
legal burden of proof;

child means a child of any age and includes the meaning given in clause 10(1)
of Part 2 of this Dictionary;

civil penalty is defined in clause 3 of Part 2 of this Dictionary;

civil proceeding means a proceeding other than a criminal proceeding;

client is defined in section 117;

coincidence evidence means evidence of a kind referred to in section 98(1) that
a party seeks to have adduced for the purpose referred to in that subsection;

coincidence rule means section 98(1);

Commonwealth owned body corporate means a body corporate that, were the
Commonwealth a body corporate, would, for the purposes of the
Corporations Act 2001 of the Commonwealth, be—

(a) a wholly-owned subsidiary of the Commonwealth; or

(b) a wholly-owned subsidiary of another body corporate that is, under this
definition, a Commonwealth owned body corporate because of the
application of paragraph (a) (including the application of that paragraph
together with another application or other applications of this paragraph);

Commonwealth record means a record made by—

(a) a Department within the meaning of the Public Service Act 1999 of the
Commonwealth; or

(b) the Parliament, a House of the Parliament, a committee of a House of
the Parliament or a committee of the Parliament; or

(c) a person or body, other than a Legislative Assembly, holding office, or
exercising power, under or because of the Commonwealth Constitution or a
law of the Commonwealth; or

(d) a body or organisation other than a Legislative Assembly, whether
incorporated or unincorporated, established for a public purpose—

(i) by or under a law of the Commonwealth or of a Territory (other than
the Australian Capital Territory, the Northern Territory or Norfolk
Island); or

(ii) by the Governor-General; or

(iii) by a Minister of the Commonwealth; or

(e) any other body or organisation that is a Commonwealth owned body
corporate—

and kept or maintained by a person, body or organisation of a kind referred to in
paragraph (a), (b), (c), (d) or (e), but does not include a record made by a
person or body holding office, or exercising power, under or because of the

Commonwealth Constitution or a law of the Commonwealth if the record was not made in connection with holding the office concerned, or exercising the power concerned;

confidential communication is defined in section 117;

confidential document is defined in section 117;

court means Victorian court;

credibility of a person who has made a representation that has been admitted in evidence means the **credibility of the representation**, and includes the person's ability to observe or remember facts and events about which the person made the representation;

credibility of a witness means the credibility of any part or all of the evidence of the witness, and includes the witness's ability to observe or remember facts and events about which the witness has given, is giving or is to give evidence;

credibility evidence is defined in section 101A;

credibility rule means section 102;

criminal proceeding means a prosecution for an offence and includes—

(a) a proceeding for the committal of a person for trial or sentence for an offence; and

(b) a proceeding relating to bail—

but does not include a prosecution for an offence that is a prescribed taxation offence within the meaning of Part III of the Taxation Administration Act 1953 of the Commonwealth;

cross-examination is defined in clause 2(2) of Part 2 of this Dictionary;

cross-examiner means a party who is cross-examining a witness;

de facto partner is defined in clause 11 of Part 2 of this Dictionary;

document means any record of information, and includes—

(a) anything on which there is writing; or

(b) anything on which there are marks, figures, symbols or perforations having a meaning for persons qualified to interpret them; or

(c) anything from which sounds, images or writings can be reproduced with or without the aid of anything else; or

(d) a map, plan, drawing or photograph;

electronic communication has the same meaning as it has in the Electronic Transactions (Victoria) Act 2000;

examination in chief is defined in clause 2(1) of Part 2 of this Dictionary;

exercise of a function includes performance of a duty;

fax, in relation to a document, means a copy of the document that has been reproduced by facsimile telegraphy;

federal court [Note- The Commonwealth Act includes a definition of this term].

foreign court means any court (including any person or body authorised to take or receive evidence, whether on behalf of a court or otherwise and whether or not the person or body is empowered to require the answering of questions or the production of documents) of a foreign country or a part of such a country;

foreign lawyer has the same meaning as it has in the Legal Profession Uniform Law (Victoria);

function includes power, authority or duty;

government or official gazette includes the Government Gazette; [Note - The definition of this term in the Commonwealth Act and New South Wales Act differs from this definition.]

Governor of a State includes any person for the time being administering the Government of the State;

Governor-General means Governor-General of the Commonwealth and includes any person for the time being administering the Government of the Commonwealth; [Note The Commonwealth Act does not include definitions of Governor of a State and Governor-General. These definitions are covered by sections 16A and 16B of the Acts Interpretation Act 1901 of the Commonwealth.

hearsay rule means section 59(1);]

identification evidence means evidence that is—

(a) an assertion by a person to the effect that an accused was, or resembles (visually, aurally or otherwise) a person who was, present at or near a place where—

(i) the offence for which the accused is being prosecuted was committed; or

(ii) an act connected to that offence was done—

at or about the time at which the offence was committed or the act was done, being an assertion that is based wholly or partly on what the person making the assertion saw, heard or otherwise perceived at that place and time; or

(b) a report (whether oral or in writing) of such an assertion;

investigating official means—

(a) a police officer (other than a police officer who is engaged in covert investigations under the orders of a superior); or

(b) a person appointed by or under an Australian law (other than a person who is engaged in covert investigations under the orders of a superior) whose functions include functions in respect of the prevention or investigation of offences;

joint sitting means—

(a) in relation to the Parliament of the Commonwealth—a joint sitting of the members of the Senate and of the House of Representatives convened by the Governor-General under section 57 of the Commonwealth Constitution or convened under any Act of the Commonwealth; or

(b) in relation to a bicameral legislature of a State—a joint sitting of both Houses of the legislature convened under a law of the State;

judge, in relation to a proceeding, means the judge, magistrate or other person before whom the proceeding is being held;

law is defined in clause 9 of Part 2 of this Dictionary;

leading question means a question asked of a witness that—

(a) directly or indirectly suggests a particular answer to the question; or

(b) assumes the existence of a fact the existence of which is in dispute in the proceeding and as to the existence of which the witness has not given evidence before the question is asked;

Legislative Assembly means any present or former Legislative Assembly of a Territory, and includes the Australian Capital Territory House of Assembly;

member of the Australian Federal Police includes a special member or a staff member of the Australian Federal Police;

non-participant registered foreign lawyer has the same meaning as it has in Schedule 3 to the Legal Profession Uniform Law (Victoria);

NSW court [Note - The New South Wales Act includes this definition.]

offence means an offence against or arising under an Australian law;

opinion rule means section 76;

parent includes the meaning given in clause 10(2) of Part 2 of this Dictionary;

picture identification evidence is defined in section 115;

police officer means—

(a) a member of the Australian Federal Police; or

(b) a member of the police force of a State or Territory;

postal article has the same meaning as in the Australian Postal Corporation Act 1989 of the Commonwealth;

previous representation means a representation made otherwise than in the course of giving evidence in the proceeding in which evidence of the representation is sought to be adduced;

prior consistent statement of a witness means a previous representation that is consistent with evidence given by the witness;

prior inconsistent statement of a witness means a previous representation that is inconsistent with evidence given by the witness;

probative value of evidence means the extent to which the evidence could rationally affect the assessment of the probability of the existence of a fact in issue;

prosecutor means a person who institutes or is responsible for the conduct of a prosecution;

public document means a document that—

(a) forms part of the records of the Crown in any of its capacities; or

(b) forms part of the records of the government of a foreign country; or

(c) forms part of the records of a person or body holding office or exercising a function under or because of the Commonwealth Constitution, an Australian law or a law of a foreign country; or

(d) is being kept by or on behalf of the Crown, such a government or such a person or body—

and includes the records of the proceedings of, and papers presented to—

(e) an Australian Parliament, a House of an Australian Parliament, a committee of such a House or a committee of an Australian Parliament; and

(f) a legislature of a foreign country, including a House or committee (however described) of such a legislature;

re-examination is defined in clause 2(3) and (4) of Part 2 of this Dictionary;

representation includes—

(a) an express or implied representation (whether oral or in writing); or

(b) a representation to be inferred from conduct; or

(c) a representation not intended by its maker to be communicated to or seen by another person; or

(d) a representation that for any reason is not communicated;

seal includes a stamp;

tendency evidence means evidence of a kind referred to in section 97(1) that a party seeks to have adduced for the purpose referred to in that subsection

tendency rule means section 97(1);

traditional laws and customs of an Aboriginal or Torres Strait Islander group (including a kinship group) includes any of the traditions, customary laws, customs, observances, practices, knowledge and beliefs of the group;

Victorian court means—

    (a) the Supreme Court; or

    (b) any other court created by Parliament—

and includes any person or body (other than a court) that, in exercising a function under the law of the State, is required to apply the laws of evidence;

visual identification evidence is defined in section 114;

witness includes the meaning given in clause 7 of Part 2 of this Dictionary.

Part 2—Other expressions

1. References to businesses

(1) A reference in this Act to a business includes a reference to the following—

    (a) a profession, calling, occupation, trade or undertaking;

    (b) an activity engaged in or carried on by the Crown in any of its capacities;

    (c) an activity engaged in or carried on by the government of a foreign country;

    (d) an activity engaged in or carried on by a person or body holding office or exercising power under or because of the Commonwealth Constitution, an Australian law or a law of a foreign country, being an activity engaged in or carried on in the performance of the functions of the office or in the exercise of the power (otherwise than in a private capacity);

    (e) the proceedings of an Australian Parliament, a House of an Australian Parliament, a committee of such a House or a committee of an Australian Parliament;

    (f) the proceedings of a legislature of a foreign country, including a House or committee (however described) of such a legislature.

(2) A reference in this Act to a business also includes a reference to—

    (a) a business that is not engaged in or carried on for profit; or

    (b) a business engaged in or carried on outside Australia.

2. References to examination in chief, cross-examination and re examination

(1) A reference in this Act to examination in chief of a witness is a reference to the questioning of a witness by the party who called the witness to give evidence, not being questioning that is re examination.

(2) A reference in this Act to cross-examination of a witness is a reference to the questioning of a witness by a party other than the party who called the witness to give evidence.

(3) A reference in this Act to re-examination of a witness is a reference to the questioning of a witness by the party who called the witness to give evidence, being questioning (other than further examination in chief with the leave of the court) conducted after the cross-examination of the witness by another party.

(4) If a party has recalled a witness who has already given evidence, a reference in this Act to re-examination of a witness does not include a reference to the questioning of the witness by that party before the witness is questioned by another party.

3. References to civil penalties

For the purposes of this Act, a person is taken to be liable to a civil penalty if, in an Australian or overseas proceeding (other than a criminal proceeding), the person would be liable to a penalty arising under an Australian law or a law of a foreign country.

4. Unavailability of persons

(1) For the purposes of this Act, a person is taken not to be available to give evidence about a fact if—

(a) the person is dead; or

(b) the person is, for any reason other than the application of section 16 (Competence and compellability—judges and jurors), not competent to give the evidence; or

(c) the person is mentally or physically unable to give the evidence and it is not reasonably practicable to overcome that inability; or

(d) it would be unlawful for the person to give the evidence; or

(e) a provision of this Act prohibits the evidence being given; or

(f) all reasonable steps have been taken, by the party seeking to prove the person is not available, to find the person or secure his or her attendance, but without success; or

(g) all reasonable steps have been taken, by the party seeking to prove the person is not available, to compel the person to give the evidence, but without success.

(2) In all other cases the person is taken to be available to give evidence about the fact.

5. Unavailability of documents and things

For the purposes of this Act, a document or thing is taken not to be available to a party if and only if—

(a) it cannot be found after reasonable inquiry and search by the party; or

(b) it was destroyed by the party, or by a person on behalf of the party, otherwise than in bad faith, or was destroyed by another person; or

(c) it would be impractical to produce the document or thing during the course of the proceeding; or

(d) production of the document or thing during the course of the proceeding could render a person liable to conviction for an offence; or

(e) it is not in the possession or under the control of the party and—

(i) it cannot be obtained by any judicial procedure of the court; or

(ii) it is in the possession or under the control of another party to the proceeding concerned who knows or might reasonably be expected to know that evidence of the contents of the document, or evidence of the thing, is likely to be relevant in the proceeding; or

(iii) it was in the possession or under the control of such a party at a time when that party knew or might reasonably be expected to have known that such evidence was likely to be relevant in the proceeding.

6. Representations in documents

For the purposes of this Act, a representation contained in a document is taken to have been made by a person if—

(a) the document was written, made or otherwise produced by the person; or

(b) the representation was recognised by the person as his or her representation by signing, initialling or otherwise marking the document.

7. Witnesses

(1) A reference in this Act to a witness includes a reference to a party giving evidence.

(2) A reference in this Act to a witness who has been called by a party to give evidence includes a reference to the party giving evidence.

(3) A reference in this clause to a party includes an accused in a criminal proceeding.

8. References to documents

A reference in this Act to a document includes a reference to—

(a) any part of the document; or

(b) any copy, reproduction or duplicate of the document or of any part of the document; or

(c) any part of such a copy, reproduction or duplicate.

8A. References to offices etc.

In this Act—

(a) a reference to a person appointed or holding office under or because of an Australian law or a law of the Commonwealth includes a reference to an APS employee within the meaning of the Public Service Act 1999 of the Commonwealth; and

(b) in that context, a reference to an office is a reference to a position occupied by the APS employee concerned, and a reference to an officer includes a reference to a Secretary, or APS employee, within the meaning of the Act.

9. References to laws

(1) A reference in this Act to a law of the Commonwealth, a State, a Territory or a foreign country is a reference to a law (whether written or unwritten) of or in force in that place.

(2) A reference in this Act to an Australian law is a reference to an Australian law (whether written or unwritten) of or in force in Australia.

10. References to children and parents

(1) A reference in this Act to a child of a person includes a reference to—

(a) an adopted child or ex-nuptial child of the person; or

(b) a child living with the person as if the child were a member of the person's family.

(2) A reference in this Act to a parent of a person includes a reference to—

(a) an adoptive parent of the person; or

(b) if the person is an ex-nuptial child—the person's natural father; or

(c) the person with whom a child is living as if the child were a member of the person's family.

11. References to de facto partners

(1) A reference in this Act to a de facto partner of a person is a reference to a person who is in a de facto relationship with the person.

(2) A person is in a de facto relationship with another person if the two persons have a relationship as a couple and are not legally married.

(3) In determining whether two persons are in a de facto relationship, all the circumstances of the relationship are to be taken into account, including such of the following matters as are relevant in the circumstances of the particular case—

(a) the duration of the relationship;

(b) the nature and extent of their common residence;

(c) the degree of financial dependence or interdependence, and any arrangements for financial support, between them;

(d) the ownership, use and acquisition of their property;

(e) the degree of mutual commitment to a shared life;

(f) the care and support of children;

(g) the reputation and public aspects of the relationship.

(4) No particular finding in relation to any circumstance is to be regarded as necessary in deciding whether two persons have a relationship as a couple.

(5) For the purposes of subclause (3), the following matters are irrelevant—

(a) whether the persons are different sexes or the same sex;

(b) whether either of the persons is legally married to someone else or in another de facto relationship.

(6) Despite subclauses (3) and (4), a person is in a de facto relationship with another person if those two persons are in a registered domestic relationship within the meaning of the Relationships Act 2008.

For a wealth of evidence resources on Victoria
see the website of the Judicial College of Victoria
https://www.judicialcollege.vic.edu.au/resources/evidence

Making and Responding to Common Objections

Professor John Barkai

> This section provides ideas about making and responding to common objections, and includes a list of common objections.

An almost endless number of objections could be made at trial. Many lists, "cheat sheets," and articles about objections can be found on the internet. This section of the book will summarize those resources, discuss the basics about objections, and provide a list of the more common objections.

Why Do Lawyers Object?
Lawyers object to:

1) limit the information fact finder can consider by excluding testimony, witnesses, or exhibits offered by the opposing party,

2) control the opposing lawyer's conduct
by preventing certain questions or answers, the calling of certain witnesses, and certain statements from being made during opening statements or closing arguments,

3) preserve errors for appeal,

4) disrupt opponent's counsel's momentum,

5) send a signal to a witness,

6) communicate with the fact finder, and

7) give the witness a break and time to think.

Lawyers frequently object to the form of question (Argumentative, Ambiguous, Vague, Asked and Answered, etc.) to prevent the judge or jury from hearing inadmissible evidence. Often, however, such objections are made simply to harass, annoy, upset, or distract opposing counsel. The less experience the lawyer has, the more such objections are likely to distract. Some people consider objections made for such purposes to be "unethical;" other people consider such objections part of the competition in the adversary system. Whatever your view, be ready for such objections.

Make an Objection in Four Steps

1) Stand up.
2) Say, "Objection ____" (Fill in the blank with your reason).
3) Identify your specific objection.
    a) At a minimum, say the topic type
        (Hearsay, Relevance, Improper Impeachment, Improper
        Character, Lack of Foundation, Leading Question, etc.)
    b) State the evidence act section number if you know it (23, 26,
etc.).
    c) A combination of the above
        ("Objection, Improper Impeachment, Section 23")
4) Stop talking and listen to the judge.
    Be prepared to state reasons for your objection and to make an
    argument to support your position.

How to Respond to an Objection

1) Speak to the judge, not the lawyer who objected.
2) Explain to the judge why your evidence should be admissible.
    ("Your Honor, that statement is not hearsay because I am not
    offering it for the truth, but rather to show notice.")
3) If you recognize that you did not lay an appropriate foundation
    for the evidence, explain that you will do that. ("Your Honor, I
    will lay the foundation.")
4) If you recognize that the opposing counsel was objecting to the
    form of your question, which most often happens on your
    direct examination, simply say, "I'll rephrase." Rephrase the
    question and move on with your witness examination. Do not
    get sidetracked by the opposing counsel who might have
    objected just to throw you off track.
5) For any physical piece of evidence, statement, or testimony that
    you will be introducing, prepare in advance and have a reason
    why you believe that evidence is admissible. Be ready to make
    that argument to the judge.
6) If the objection is to relevance, and you think you will be able to
    show that it is relevant after additional testimony, say to the
    judge, "I will connect it up in a few questions Your Honor."
    Such a statement is equivalent of saying "trust me." If you do
    say that, you had better connect it up later or else the judge will
    later strike your evidence and will not trust you in the future.

If You are a Judge Who Has to Rule on the Objection
1) If the specific objection was not identified, turn to the lawyer who made the objection and say, "Basis?" - Meaning, "What is the legal basis for your objection?"
2) After the lawyer has put their specific objection on the record, turn to the proponent (the lawyer who is attempting to introduce the evidence), and say, "What is your response?"
3) Allow more argument if necessary. "Counsel, how do you respond to that argument?"
4) After the arguments are completed, make your ruling.
    A) "Sustained" - meaning you agree with the objection, and you will exclude the evidence.
    B) "Overruled" - meaning you agree with the proponent of the evidence, and the evidence will be admissible.
    C) Reserve your ruling until the end of the trial. ("I will reserve my decision on this issue until the close of the testimony.")
    D) Ask lawyers to submit a written memorandum on the issue so you have a better understanding of the issue, the law, and the precedent.

Multiple Lawyers and Multiple Clients
If two or more lawyers represent one client, only one of the lawyers can object to each witness, e.g. if you do the direct, you are the only one who can object on cross. Co-counsel for the same party cannot both object or respond to objections for single witness. If there are multiple parties who each have their own lawyer, each lawyer must make their own objection to have the objections preserved for appeal.

Judges Apply the Rules of Evidence More Loosely in Nonjury Trials. Many jurisdictions seem to apply a presumption that a trial judge will ignore inadmissible evidence in a non-jury trial. Questionable evidence is very seldom basis for reversing a verdict in a nonjury trial.

The Key to Objections is FRE 103 There is a rhyme to this phrase. "Key" rhymes with "103." Rule 103 holds the key to understanding the process of objections. Read that rule very carefully.

FRE 103. Rulings on Evidence

(a) Preserving a Claim of Error. A party may claim error in a ruling to admit or exclude evidence only if the error affects a substantial right of the party and:

    (1) if the ruling admits evidence, a party, on the record:

        (A) timely objects or moves to strike; and

        (B) states the specific ground, unless it was apparent from the context; or

    (2) if the ruling excludes evidence, a party informs the court of its substance by an offer of proof, unless the substance was apparent from the context.

(b) Not Needing to Renew an Objection or Offer of Proof. Once the court rules definitively on the record — either before or at trial — a party need not renew an objection or offer of proof to preserve a claim of error for appeal.

(c) Court's Statement About the Ruling; Directing an Offer of Proof. The court may make any statement about the character or form of the evidence, the objection made, and the ruling. The court may direct that an offer of proof be made in question-and-answer form.

(d) Preventing the Jury from Hearing Inadmissible Evidence. To the extent practicable, the court must conduct a jury trial so that inadmissible evidence is not suggested to the jury by any means.

(e) Taking Notice of Plain Error. A court may take notice of a plain error affecting a substantial right, even if the claim of error was not properly preserved.

Important Points about Rule 103 include:

1) The objection must be timely and state the specific ground for the objection, unless it is apparent from the context.

2) If the evidence was admitted, appellate courts do not have to consider the issue unless a specific ground for the objection was timely stated.

3) If the evidence was excluded, the appellate court needs information about what the excluded evidence was going to be. That information must be provided by an "offer of proof" unless the information was apparent from the context.

4) The judge can make statements for the record about the objection, the evidence, the form of the evidence, the ruling, and can require an offer of proof in question and answer form.

5) An error is not sufficient to reverse the trial unless a "substantial right" of a party is affected.

6) Even if there was no objection at trial, "plain errors" affecting "substantial rights" can result in a reversal on appeal.

The Most Common Substantive Objections Are Based on The Rules of Evidence and Constitutional Issues.

Each article within the evidence code has one or more common types of objections, such as: FRE

General provisions   100s
    Objections
    Preliminary questions
    Limited admissibility
    Remainder of or related writings
Judicial notice   200s
Presumptions   300s
Relevance   400s
Privileges   500s
Witnesses   600s
    Competence
    Impeachment
Opinions and expert testimony   700s
Hearsay   800s
Authentication   900s
Best evidence (original writings) 1000s

Motions in Limine

In countries with jury trials, a lawyer may make a pretrial motion in limine, which is a motion to exclude or admit certain evidence prior to trial. In jury trials, the motion is made outside the presence of the jury. The judge's ruling on the motion in limine can 1) prevent inadmissible evidence from being heard by a jury, or 2) allow lawyers to know that they can go forward and attempt to introduce certain evidence without risking a mistrial. Motions in limine are probably not necessary in a nonjury trial because the judge will have to hear the potentially inadmissible evidence before ruling on the motion. Therefore, even if the evidence would be ruled inadmissible, the trial judge who will be the trier of fact will have already heard the inadmissible evidence. Judges in nonjury trials are presumed to ignore inadmissible evidence.

Phrases and Questions that Suggest Inadmissible or Objectionable Information is Coming.

Lawyer: "In summary, witness you've testified that…"
Likely objection: Asked and answered

Lawyer: "Witness, what if I told you that another witness testified that…"
Likely objection: Calls for speculation, argumentative, etc.

Inadequate Objections – Not Specific Enough
"I object."
"Objection to the form of the question."
"Insufficient foundation."
"Inadmissible."
"Incompetent, irrelevant, and immaterial."

Offers of Proof are:
1) sometimes just summary statements by a lawyer of what the evidence would be if the lawyer were given an opportunity to call the witness or introduce the exhibit. ("Your Honor, if the witness would be allowed to testify, she would say that ……"), and,
2) sometimes offers of proof are questions of the lawyer and answers of the witness given in question and answer form outside the presence of the jury. (Q1 A1; Q2 A2; Q3 A3)

The Impact of Objections in Nonjury Trials – Seldom Reversed

Objections to the form of questions seldom result in reversals even in jury trials. Furthermore, it is extremely rare for an appellate court to reverse a nonjury trial decision based on an objection to the form of a question or the form of an answer. Objection battles on the forms of questions are less important in nonjury trials because the judge in a non-jury trial is presumed to ignore inadmissible evidence and decide the case only on evidence that was admissible.

Common Phrases from Court Opinions Summarizing That Inadmissible Evidence in A Nonjury Trial Will Not Result in A Reversal Include:

- "Trial judges often have access to inadmissible and highly prejudicial information and are presumed to be able to discount or disregard it."
- "In bench (non-jury trials, judges routinely hear inadmissible evidence that they are presumed to ignore."
- "The presumption that the trial judge disregarded all inadmissible evidence in reaching his decision."
- "It is presumed that improper evidence taken under objection was given no weight in reaching the final conclusion in a nonjury trial unless the contrary appears."
- "A judge, as factfinder, is presumed to disregard inadmissible evidence and consider only competent evidence."
- "A judge "must be presumed to be able to disregard inflammatory evidence"

Common Objections to the Form of the Question

Objections to the form of the question often have no clear answers or standards. Many judges and lawyers might disagree as to whether some question is improper or not. If a rule is cited when making the objection, it would usually be FRE 611.

Argumentative (also called **Harassing, Badgering**)
An argumentative question asks the witness to accept the examiner's summary, inference, or conclusion rather than a fact. Often the objector is trying to protect a witness during cross-examination.
Examples of Argumentative Questions:
    "Isn't what you told this judge on its face ridiculous?"
    "How can you expect the judge to believe that?"
    "Are you telling this court that you don't know what a machete is?"
    "Do you really expect the judge to believe that?"
    "Do you mean to tell me...?"
    "Doesn't it seem strange that...?"
    "Your kind of the hatchet man down here for the D.A.s Office, aren't you?"
    "It wouldn't bother you any, to come in here and lie from the time you started to the time you stopped, would it?"

Asked and Answered: This rule is violated by repeating the same question, asked by the same lawyer, to get the same answer, from the same witness. A question which has previously been asked and answered is being asked again. The rule prevents cumulative testimony FRE403. Similar questions are permitted if the identical information is not repeated. This objection does not apply to prevent the same questions being asked on cross-examination that were asked on direct examination by opposing counsel. It does not prevent asking identical questions of different witnesses, nor does it prevent a lawyer representing a co-party from asking the same questions to the same witness again.

Assuming Facts Not in Evidence. This rule is violated when part of a question (usually the first part) assumes the truth of a fact that is in dispute but has not yet been proved at trial. Such a question is unfair because it cannot be answered without conceding the unproven fact. Assuming facts not in evidence may be an attempt to bring into the trial information that the lawyer is not able to prove by other means. However, questions that assume facts are permitted on cross-examination to impeach a witness's credibility.

Examples of assuming facts not in evidence:

> "When did you stop beating your wife?" (assumes previous beatings)
>
> "Did you know their business dropped 50% because of what the defendant did?" (assumes the defendant did the same thing)
>
> "How long after you purchased the items were they given to the defendant?" (assumes the purchase)

Responses:

"I will connect it up later."(Which just means, "Judge trust me and allow a few more questions." If you request permission to "connect up later," you'd better be able to connect it up or the judge will no longer trust you.)

> "I have a good faith basis for assuming those facts. I would like to proceed without further tipping my hand."
>
> "This is criminal case and the defendant has a constitutional right to fully cross-examine the witness."

Beyond the Scope (of a prior direct of cross examination)

Questions on redirect examination cannot go into subject matters that have not been covered in the previous cross-examination. Similarly, questions on re-cross examination cannot go beyond the scope of redirect examination. Redirect examination is limited to issues raised by the opposing lawyer on cross-examination. If the questions go beyond the issues raised on cross, the objection will be valid.

Responses.

> "Your Honor, I'm allowed to go into this area because it goes to the witness's credibility."

Note well: Cross-examination is not limited to the subjects covered on direct examination. If it were so limited, the cross examiner would be prohibited from fully examining the witness and exposing weaknesses in the direct exam. If a "beyond the scope" objection is raised to a cross-examination question, the best response probably would be, "Your Honor, FRE611 allows me to cross on the subject matter of direct examination and "matters affecting the witness's credibility." My cross goes to credibility."

Compound Questions

A compound question has two or more separate questions in a single question, and usually contains the words "and" or "or." A simple "yes" or "no" answer to the question will be unclear. If the witness asked answers "yes" or "no," it is not clear if the "yes" or "no" applies to all the multiple parts of the question or just one part.

Examples:

"On that day, you went shopping <u>and</u> to the beach, didn't you?"

"Did you determine the time of death by interviewing witnesses <u>and</u> by requesting the autopsy report?"

"On Saturday, did you send the email <u>and</u> also call him?"

Cumulative

Cumulative questions ask for the same information from the same witness multiple times (like asked and answered) or ask multiple witnesses for the same information to establish the same facts.

Lack of (or insufficient) Foundation

A lack of foundation objection is proper when the lawyer asks a question before establishing the preliminary facts which would permit the questions. The evidence lacks testimony as to its authenticity or source.

Example:

"My partner saw Watkins stumble inside Cut-Rate Liquor store."

"Objection: Lack of personal knowledge – and hearsay."

Leading Question

A leading question improperly suggests the answer that the lawyer wants from the witness. Another definition is that a leading question contains the desired answer. The danger is that a leading question will make the witness agree with a false suggestion.

Often leading questions start with phrases like - "Isn't it true that…" "Did…?" or ends with "…,right?" Questions that start with the word "So" should be at least a yellow flag that the question might be leading. Although some questions are obviously leading, lawyers and judges often have different interpretations of what a leading question is. Be prepared to quickly rephrase your question if an objection to it is sustained to your question. Whether or not a question that contains the phrase "whether or not" is leading has been subject to much debate. A lawyer's nonverbal behavior or voice inflection is sometimes considered when determining whether a question is leading.

Leading is generally not permitted on direct examination. However, leading is allowed and in fact expected when cross examining a witness called by the opposing party.

Leading questions are permissible for preliminary matters, when a party calls a hostile witness or an adverse witness (FRE 611) or when a witness is very young, very old, or mentally challenged. Leading questions are also common and proper on direct examination when laying foundations because under FRE 104 the rules of evidence do not apply, except for privileges, when asking preliminary questions about the admissibility of evidence. Leading questions are also permissible when they are used like a topic sentence in a paragraph to move a witness on direct examination to another part of the scene. For example," Did there come a time when you went into the store?" Of course, the lawyer could get the same result by simply making the statement, "Now I want to ask you some questions about what you did when you went into the store." It is a common belief that the more a lawyer leads on direct examination, the less credibility the witness will have because the witness looks like they are being told what to say during the examination.

Motion to strike

Motions to strike are used two ways. First, U.S. Rule of Civil Procedure 12(f) allows for motions to strike certain pleadings. Second, Motions to strike, under evidence R103, are treated similarly to objections and ask the judge to strike inadmissible testimony from the record if the witness has just said the objectionable words. Of course, "striking" is not really striking. The inadmissible words are not removed from the court records but remain in the record even if the testimony is "stricken." The opposing lawyer can ask the judge to instruct the jury to disregard the "stricken" testimony, but psychologically, such an instruction to "disregard" the testimony might highlight the testimony for the jury. Tough choices to make.

Narrative Question, or Calls for A Narrative Answer, or simply Narrative Answer

A narrative objection can refer to a question that asks a witness to tell a story rather than to state only a few specific facts, or refer to witness' answer which is several sentences, or even paragraphs, long. On one hand, narrative answers allow the witness to easily include inadmissible evidence, but on the other hand, a narrative story might more likely provide truthful facts.

Examples of narrative questions:

"What did you do that day?"

"Tell us about the accident."

"Now tell us what everyone said and did at that point."

"What happened that night?"

"How did the accident happen?"

Ans: "First thing I got up and I... Then I went to... After that I ... She told me that... And I immediately saw the ..."

Non-Responsive Answer: The non-responsive answer objection is made to an answer that does not answer the question that was asked. Simply, the witness does not answer the question asked by the lawyer. Often the witness is trying to make their own point and take control of the testimony. A problem with nonresponsive answers is that the witness is volunteering information that might be irrelevant or unfairly prejudicial. <u>In theory, only the lawyer asking the question can object to a non-responsive answer.</u> Some judges will only allow this objection from the lawyer who is asking the question. If the objection is sustained, it is often followed by a motion to strike the answer from the record. If the opposing lawyer is considering making a non-responsive answer objection, they should consider making some other appropriate objection such as "irrelevant," "unfairly prejudicial," or "lack of foundation."

Example of a non-responsive answers:

Q: "Did you see the other driver get out of his car right after the accident?"

A: "He told me he had insurance." (non-responsive)

Q: "Weren't you the last person the victim saw on the night of his death?"

A: "I had nothing to do with that!" (non-responsive)

Speculation – Calls for Speculation – Lack Person Knowledge.
A speculation objection is proper if the lawyer asks the witness a question that the witness has no personal knowledge about, or the witness testifies about something they have not perceived. A red flag signaling a call for speculation is often a question that starts with, Isn't it possible that...?" A better phrasing to accomplish the same objective would be to focus the question on the witness's personal knowledge and experience by asking for the same information but stating it as follows, "You don't know whether or not..., do you?"
Examples of a question calling for speculation:
"What do you think he was thinking about at that time?"
"Why would she do something like that?"

Vague and Ambiguous Question: Vague and ambiguous questions are asked in ways that are incomprehensible, incomplete, or the answer will be ambiguous. If you, as the opposing lawyer, do not understand the question asked by your opponent, then the witness probably does not understand the question either. Object.

Other Objections

Golden Rule
The Golden Rule objection is made when the opposing counsel places the trier of fact (judge or jury) in the same situation that the case is about.
Examples of a Golden Rule objection:
"Your Honor, what would you have done in a situation like that?"
"Ladies and gentlemen of the jury, would you want someone like that coming into your neighborhood?"

Speaking Objections

A speaking objection is a lawyer's attempt to influence the jury by speaking to the jury by using the objection. Although such objections are very disfavored by judges in jury trials, in nonjury trials such objections can be used to make an argument to the trial judge and influence the decision to be made on the objection.

Examples of speaking objections:

"Well Judge, I am going to strongly object to this procedure. I feel that I am being sandbagged here and I don't appreciate it."

"Your honor, it doesn't matter what the answer is. Opposing counsel just wants to make a statement. He doesn't care what this witness says."

Coaching the witness

Such objections can be used to communicate with and coach a witness.

Example of coaching the witness through an objection:

"Objection. The witness couldn't possibly know that answer."
Witness then responds by saying, "I don't know."

Relevance

Questions in a case about some other person, some other event, and some other time, are irrelevant unless the judge find such questions to be relevant in this particular case for a special reason such as to show bias or relevant in this case under FRE 404(b). I call such irrelevant evidence P.E.T. evidence and tell my students that PET evidence is not admissible - evidence about some other Person, or Event, or Time. Furthermore, questions about "**what most people do**" are almost always irrelevant.

Examples of irrelevant "what most people do" objections:

"Don't most people know that…?"

"Don't most people speed when their car is headed downhill?"

A Few Useful Definitions

Stipulation: Agreement between opposing lawyers to admit certain evidence without the normal in-court proof. The trier of fact then assumes the fact to have been proven.

Offer of Proof: A statement by a lawyer describing evidence that the lawyer wants admitted. Proponent summarizes the substance of the excluded evidence to the judge to persuade the judge and to make a record for appeal.

Motion in Limine:
A pre-trial motion seeking a ruling to admit or exclude evidence.

Limited Admissibility:
Evidence can be admitted for one purpose or against one party, but not admitted for another purpose or against another party.

Intrinsic Impeachment: The impeaching statement comes out of the witness' own mouth on cross-examination. After direct exam, a witness is impeached on cross.

Extrinsic Impeachment: With extrinsic impeachment, the impeaching statement or information comes from another witness or from use of a document to impeach. If a witness is not impeached on cross by the opponent's questions (which is called intrinsic impeachment), not all types of impeachment are permitted by extrinsic impeachment. The most common limitation is FRE 608(b) prohibiting the use of extrinsic evidence of prior bad acts related to dishonestly.

Collateral Evidence: Evidence that is not relevant to the main or material issues at trial and is only relevant to a witness' credibility is called "collateral."

Collateral Matter Rule: An opposing party may not use extrinsic evidence (meaning calling another witness or using a document) to impeach a witness on a collateral matter. Bias, perception, memory, capacity and prior convictions (under FRE 609) are always material and never collateral. Bad acts of untruthfulness under FRE 608(b) are always collateral and not admissible. Prior inconsistent statements and contradictory facts may be collateral if the impeaching facts does not relate to an outcome effecting fact and are being used only for impeaching credibility of the witness.

A List of Common Possible Objections

Ambiguous	Improper opinion
Argumentative	Improper rehabilitation
Asked and answered	Inadmissible opinion
Assumes facts not in evidence	Incompetent witness
Authentication	Incomplete Inflammatory
Badgering	Insufficient foundation
Best evidence	Irrelevant (Relevance)
Beyond the scope	Lack of foundation
Bias	Lack of personal knowledge
Bolstering	Leading question
Calls for a conclusion	Misleading
Calls for speculation	Misquotes a witness or exhibit
Chain of custody	Misquotes evidence
Collateral	Misstates witness
Competence	More prejudicial than
Compound question	probative
Compromise / Settlement offer	Motion to strike
Confrontation (lack of)	Narrative
Confusing	(Question calls for a narrative)
Counsel is testifying	Narrative answer
Cumulative	Non-responsive
Document speaks for itself	Nothing pending
Expert (Improper opinion)	Outside the scope of cross
Expert (not qualified)	Overly broad or general
Habit	Parole evidence rule
Harassing the witness	Personal knowledge
Hearsay	Prejudice (unfair)
Hypothetical question misused	Privilege communication
Improper character evidence	Relevance
Improper characterization	Speculation/ Opinion/ Lack of
Improper impeachment	personal knowledge
	Unintelligible
	Vague

There are many more possible objections,
limited only by the lawyer's imagination.

Judges and the local legal culture in your jurisdiction may have
other rules or approaches to objections that are not discussed in
this book. Ask around and learn about them.

Evidentiary Foundations

Foundations - Predicates - Laying the Foundation

Foundations are questions asked by a lawyer to set the groundwork (the foundation) for admitting evidence at trial. The asking of these questions is often referred to as "**laying the foundation**" for the evidence. The word "**predicates,**" when used by trial lawyers, refers to a series of form or sample questions that a lawyer must ask to establish the facts, events, or conditions which are required by the rules of evidence or caselaw before presenting other evidence. Predicates are the questions that are asked when laying the foundation for other evidence. The evidentiary foundation is like the foundation for a building. It provides a solid basis for building up the structure of the case at trial. The necessary foundational questions are not always obvious by reading the rules of evidence.

Foundations may come from local legal culture - "That's the way we do things in this jurisdiction," or from a lawyer or judge's prior experience - "That's the way I was taught to do it," or "That's what I think works best," or "That's what I am requiring you to do."

Bare-Bones Foundations

The foundations provided in this book are designed to be brief - what I call "bare-bones foundations." A **bare-bones** foundation uses the minimum necessary questions to admit a piece of evidence or testimony and is less concerned about the "weight" of the evidence to be admitted. Bare-bones foundations are commonly used in non-jury trials, therefore such foundations might be very appropriate in Victorian trials. On the other hand, what I call **"advocacy foundations"** are more common in jury trials where a jury of laypeople will make the important factual determinations in the case. Because the lay jury members are not familiar with trial procedures asking more questions might improve the persuasiveness of your evidence. An advocacy foundation uses more than the bare minimum number of questions to lay the foundation, with additional questions going to enhance the persuasiveness of the sponsoring witness and the evidence.

For example, when using a police officer's report to refresh memory, or for recorded recollection, or to impeach, the additional questions might include questions relating to the training or conduct of the officer, such as:

> "Did you have training in writing reports?"
> "How much training?"
> "When you are writing your report, you knew that your supervisor will read some of your reports?"
> "You know that your future assignments might depend on the quality of your written reports?"
> "Do you reread your report before submitting it?"
> "Do you check your report for accuracy before submitting it?"

Admissibility v. Weight

Foundations are sometimes necessary for evidence to be admissible. As such, they go to the issue of "**admissibility**," which is about "can" the evidence be included in the trial so that the trier of fact (judge or jury) can consider that evidence in decision-making. On the other hand, the "**weight**" of evidence is the "value" to be given to the piece of evidence by the trier of fact. Trial judgments are usually determined by which party's admitted evidence is more persuasive, and whether the party met the burden of persuasion to the necessary standard (such as: "preponderance of the evidence" or "beyond a reasonable doubt").

Example of Admissibility and Weight

Assume the trial is about a fight. One person says, "He hit me." The other person says, "I did not." Both statements will be admissible. But after listening to the two witnesses as well as other facts and witnesses, the trier of fact will probably assign different weights or values to the testimony of the two people. Typically, one person will be considered more credible or believable than the other person. The more reliable a person's testimony seems to the trier of fact, the more it is said to be given greater weight. It is that weight of the evidence that will eventually lead to a decision for one party or the other. A common statement made by a judge when an opposing party argues against the admissibility of testimony or other evidence is, "That goes to weight, not admissibility." Such a statement by a judge means, "You just lost your battle to exclude that evidence from the trial, but you can still argue that your case is stronger and more persuasive than your opponent's case is."

3 Simple Questions

After handing a physical item to a witness and saying for the record,

"Let me show you what has been marked as proposed exhibit number one,"

the foundation for some physical pieces of evidence can be established with as few as three questions:

---

1) Q: What is it?

2) Q: How do you know that?

3) Q: Is it in the same condition as it was on the day of ...?"

(Or "Is that a fair and accurate representation of the item as it was on [a certain date]?").

Steps for Introducing Exhibits

> **Preliminary steps are:**
>
> **1) Have the exhibit marked for identification**
> **2) Show the proposed exhibit to opposing counsel**
> **3) Ask permission to approach the witness with the proposed exhibit**

1. History - How the witness knows the exhibit.

Offer some testimony that the witness <u>knows</u> or is <u>familiar with</u> the evidence – such as a document, physical item, photo, diagram, scene, text message, email - or recalls the statement. Even if the witness has only seen the exhibit once before or has just been to the scene shown in the photograph once before, <u>once is enough</u>.

2. The litany (a ritualistic repetition of foundational questions)

a) **Ask the court clerk to mark the item** (using numbers or letters). The clerk will decide which system to use. In more serious cases in the jurisdiction's higher courts (typically where jury trials are allowed), exhibits are usually required to be marked at least before trial starts, and often during pretrial conferences.

b) **Show opposing counsel** (this will prevent interruptions) and say, "Let the record reflect that I am showing the defense what has been marked as plaintiff's proposed exhibit number one."

c) **Ask the judge for permission to approach the witness**. "May I approach the witness?"

- **Q:** "**I show you what has been marked as** Plaintiff's (Prosecution's) (Defense's) proposed exhibit # x (or exhibit #x for identification purposes) **and ask whether you can identify it**" (You expect a "yes" answer here.)

- **Q:** "**What is it?**" (They describe it in general terms. "It is the contract/photo of the scene/weapon recovered/drugs seized/diagram of the area/etc.")

- **Q:** "**How do you know that?**" ("I recognize it. It has my signature on it. / I have been there many times before. / I put my initials on it and the defendant's name/etc.")

3. Show Condition or Comparison or Accuracy

Some comparison must be made between the exhibit in court and when the witness became familiar with the exhibit out-of-court. Of the examples that follow, only one such question is necessary.

- "Is this in the **same condition** as when you... [first saw it...seized it...etc.]?"
- "Is this in the **same or substantially** the same condition.... as when you..." (for item or document)
- "Is it a **fair and accurate representation** of the X **as it was that day**?" (for diagram or pictures)
- "**Has it changed** in any significant way?"
- "**How does it compare** to the item you saw that day?"

4. Move or Offer the Exhibit into Evidence

"Your honor, **I offer the exhibit into evidence**."

- or "I move the exhibit into evidence."

You could instead say, "I offer proposed exhibit # 1 into evidence as exhibit # 1," but why make it so confusing? Just say, "I offer the exhibit into evidence."

The judge <u>might</u> ask the opposing counsel, "Any objections?"

but if there is an objection to the admissibility (not the weight), the opponent should object immediately after the proponent offers the exhibit.

The judge should allow "voir dire" (immediate cross examination limited to the foundation and the admissibility) by the opponent of the exhibit.

The Common Evidentiary Foundations

(You should be able to do all of these in your sleep)

Physical Items
Photograph (printed)
Diagram of scene
Physical item seized at scene

Common Documents
Refreshing memory
Recorded recollection
Business records in paper
Business records
Deposition impeachment (see below)

Records and Treatises
Public record
Learned treatise –
      Use on direct supporting your expert
      Use on cross attacking their expert

Digital Evidence – from the internet, a cell phone, or a computer
      Also called - ESI – Electronically Stored Information
Emails
Text message – issues of incompleteness
Social Media - Facebook, Instagram, Twitter, Snapchat
Website posting
Voicemail recording
Videos, including on cell phone
Photo on cell phone
Fax
Chatroom conversations

Impeachment
      Impeaching by Prior Written Inconsistent statement
      Impeaching by Omission in Prior Written Statement
      Impeaching by Prior Oral Inconsistent statement
      Impeaching by Inconsistent Oral Deposition Transcript

Phrases to Move Evidence into a Trial

(Pick one and always use it)

"I offer the exhibit into evidence." (By far the easiest to use)

"Your Honor, I ask that what's been previously marked as Plaintiff's Exhibit A for Identification be admitted into evidence as Plaintiff's A." (Unnecessarily complex and you are likely to mess it up.)

"At this time, we offer Plaintiff's A for identification into evidence as Plaintiff's exhibit A."

"The Government at this time, would move to introduce Government's Exhibit No. 2 into evidence."

"Your Honor, we'd offer Defense Exhibit B into evidence."

"Your Honor, I move that Plaintiff's Exhibit 3 be introduced into evidence."

"We offer Exhibit A into evidence."

"Your Honor, I would like to submit People's exhibit 'A' into evidence."

"We would ask the Court to admit State's Exhibit 4 for Identification as State's 4."

Useful Points to Remember

Offering something "into evidence" means that in a jury trial the exhibit can go into the jury room and be reviewed as many times as the jurors want to look at it.

Make an Offer of Proof – if your evidence is not admitted. R103.

Hearsay within hearsay – statements incorporated into other statements need an additional hearsay exception to be admissible. R805 Hearsay Within Hearsay.

Public records do not have to be "open to the public" but rather are reports and records created by public (government) employees. R803(8)

A record automatically generated by a computer - is not hearsay (computer generated records). No assertion by a person.

Email offered to show notice, knowledge, or fear are not assertions and therefore not hearsay. In a contract or consent form, the words have independent legal significance, which means they operate to form a contract even if they are not true.

Demonstrative evidence – demonstrates or represents some real evidence. Also sometimes called **illustrative evidence**, as compared to **real evidence**, which as some historical connection to the case - such as being the drugs, the gun, etc.

A "chain of custody" is required for fungible items that cannot be identified and distinguished on sight, such as drugs, alcohol, and blood samples. They are as indistinguishable as grains of sand. Often, they are taken into custody and sent to a laboratory for testing. The "chain" makes sure the evidence that is tested is connected to the correct case.

Distinctive characteristics. Evidence tags with initials and case names make items unique and should qualify as a **"Distinctive characteristic"** under FRE 901(b)(4) for authentication purposes.

The most common methods to introduce physical and documentary evidence are **using personal knowledge and distinctive characteristics.** R901(b)(1)&(4)

Affidavits are hearsay and not admissible at trial. However, affidavits can be used in summary judgment proceedings if the statements in the affidavits would be admissible in court if testified to by the declarant with personal knowledge. Therefore, lawyers should not be sign affidavits for summary judgement. Potential witnesses with personal knowledge of the facts must sign the affidavits.

HARROWing - a Barkai acronym formed from the first letters of evidence concepts most likely to impact admissibility decisions. Always think of HARROWing when a physical item is going to be introduced, especially if the item is a document or a physical item with words on it. **H**earsay FRE 800s, **A**uthentication FRE 900s, **R**elevance FRE 401, **R**elevance FRE 403, **O**riginal **W**ritings (Best Evidence) FRE 1000s. HARROWing also applies to ESI (Electronically Stored Information) such as emails, texts, websites, etc.

OTP - what is the evidence "Offered to Prove?" OTP impacts relevance, admissibility, and the necessary foundation.

The rules of evidence do not tell you how to introduce exhibits although some rules do list the foundational elements which must be included in foundational questions. The hearsay exceptions of Recorded Recollection FRE 803(5) and Records of a Regular Conducted Activity (business records) FRE 803(6) are examples of hearsay exceptions that are so complicated that a novice trial lawyer might want to have the rule in front of them when attempting to lay the foundation.

Laying a foundation is like a sport. Practice before the game.

Steps: Mark/Pre-Mark, Show, Approach, Foundational Questions, Offer
> **Mark exhibits.** Have the exhibit marked before trial or prior to trial – depending on the court rules.

Magic Words: **"in the same or substantially the same condition"** or **"fair and accurate representation,"** or **"fairly accurate representation,"** or **"fairly represent**."

Speak in generic terms when talking about exhibits until the witness identifies the exhibit: "Proposed exhibit # 1" or "Exhibit # 1 for identification purposes," not "Your report," or "Photo of the scene."

To "publish" an exhibit means to show the exhibit to the jury or ask the judge to look at the exhibit right now, not at the end of the trial.

Chain of evidence is usually only necessary for fungible items (identical items; they all look the same), or items that need testing – drugs, alcohol, blood, DNA. Not every "kink in the link" of the chain of evidence makes evidence inadmissible. Authentication only requires production of evidence "sufficient to support a finding," R901(a)(1), which is a low standard.

Basic tasks that every trial lawyer should be able to do
- introduce documents, physical items, photographs
- refresh memory (almost always done on direct)
- use the recollection recorded hearsay exception (almost always done on direct).
- impeach (almost always done on cross); inconsistent statements & omissions.

The Best Foundation Resources
- Grimm, Joseph & Capra, Best Practices for Authenticating Digital Evidence 69 Baylor L.R. 1 (2017)
- Evidentiary Foundations for Government Attorneys (2015) (from National Attorneys General Training & Research Institute) - (JB: It contains many simple foundations.)
- Edward Imwinkelried, Evidentiary Foundations, (10th ed. 2018) – (The classic source for foundations, but less than you might want about ESI foundations, and more than you might want in the middle of trial.)
- Deanne Siemer, Laying Foundations and Meeting Objections (4th ed. 2013)

Important Evidence Rules to Guide You

FRE 103(c) Directing an Offer of Proof. – explains how to protect the record for appeal if your evidence is excluded at trial.

FRE 104 Preliminary questions.
(a) In General. In [deciding preliminary questions] the court is <u>not bound by evidence rules</u> except those on privilege.
　[**Barkai says:** that means <u>you can lead on direct for foundations.</u>]
(b) Relevance that Depends on a Fact. When the relevance of evidence depends on whether a fact exists, proof must be introduced <u>sufficient to support a finding</u> that the fact does exist.
　[**Barkai says:** <u>that is a low threshold.</u>]

FRE 901 Authenticating or Identifying Evidence.
(a) In General. To satisfy the requirement of authenticating or identifying an item of evidence, the proponent must produce <u>evidence sufficient to support a finding</u> that the item is what the proponent claims it is. [**Barkai says:** <u>that is a low threshold</u>]
(b) Examples. The following are examples only —
　(1) Testimony of a Witness with Knowledge. Testimony that an item is what it is claimed to be.
　(4) Distinctive Characteristics and the Like. The appearance, contents, substance, internal patterns, or other <u>distinctive characteristics</u> of the item, <u>taken together with all the circumstances.</u>
　(7) Evidence About Public Records.
　(9) Evidence About a Process or System.

FRE 612 Writing Used to Refresh a Witness's Memory.
Witness does not need to be the author. Anything can be used to refresh memory - even "my left shoe," which is my in-class example.

FRE 613 Witness's Prior Statement. Impeachment by inconsistent statements and omissions.

FRE 801(d)(1) Not Hearsay: A Declarant-Witness's Prior Statement. (Inconsistent under oath, consistent, or prior ID)

FRE 803(6) Records of a Regularly Conducted Activity
(JB: <u>business records are</u> **KRAP)**
　(<u>K</u>ept in the course, <u>R</u>egular practice, <u>A</u>t or near the time, <u>P</u>ersonal knowledge)

FRE 902 Evidence That Is Self-Authenticating

FRE 902(11) Certified Domestic Records of a Regularly Conducted Activity. [Note: There are many certification forms available on the internet. At least 32 states have adopted this 2002 FRE amendment.]

FRE 902(13) Certified Records Generated by an Electronic Process or System. [Only 9 states had adopted this 2017 FRE amendment.]

FRE 902(14) Certified Data Copied from an Electronic Device, Storage Medium, or File. [Only 9 states had adopted this 2017 FRE amendment.]

FRE 105 Limited Admissibility (admitted against only one party or for a limited purpose)
Only 3 states and the District of Columbia have no rule or statute similar to R105 and rely on case law (Massachusetts, Missouri, and New York).

FRE 106 Remainder of / related writing [Barkai says this means to admit the remainder now]. Only 4 states have no rule or statute (Kansas, Massachusetts, Missouri, and New York).

FRE 1006 Summaries…voluminous writings which cannot conveniently be examined in court.

The Opponent Has the Burden
On the Issue of Trustworthiness of Records

Since this 2014 FRE amendment, the burden of showing a record lacks trustworthiness is on the opponent in the Federal rules – FRE 803(6)(7)(8) …"and, <u>the opponent does not show …a lack of trustworthiness.</u>"

Only 8 of the 50 U.S. states have also amended their rules placing the burden of showing that the source of the source of information or other circumstances indicate a lack of trustworthiness on the opponent (Arizona, Mississippi, New Hampshire, New Mexico, Oregon, South Dakota, Utah, and West Virginia).

Basic Foundations & Impeachment Examples

Several of the following foundation and impeachment examples are based upon the facts of

NITA Liquor Commission v. Cut-Rate Liquor and Jones*

In this famous, fictional case from NITA (National Institute of Trial Advocacy), Walter Watkins was observed going into the Cut-Rate Liquor Store by Officer Bier and his partner from their unmarked car which was parked across the street from the liquor store. The officers had a partial view into the store and saw Watkins appear to purchase liquor at the counter. Watkins was arrested outside the store as he was leaving with a brown paper bag which contained a bottle of Thunderbird Wine. Cut-Rate Liquors and the clerk Dan Jones were issued citations for selling liquor to a person under the influence of liquor.

* This NITA Liquor Problem is used with the permission of the National Institute of Trial Advocacy (NITA). The terms "Officer Bier, Thunderbird Wine, Jackson & 7th Street, April 5th, Walter Watkins, and shoulders up" used in this publication are original to the Nita Liquor Commission v. Cut-Rate Liquor and Jones problem from *Problems in Trial Advocacy* by Donald H. Beskind and Anthony J. Bocchino, published by the National Institute of Trial Advocacy. The basis of the NITA Liquor problem and the specified terms are used here with permission.

NITA Liquor Commission
v.
Jones

The Facts

This case is a civil action brought by the Liquor
Commission against Dan Jones and the Cut-Rate Liquor
Store for civil penalties, including possible revocation of
Cut-Rate's liquor license. Investigator Bier is a typical
investigator-police officer and has investigated many
such incidents. Bier's official report appears on the next
page along with a diagram of the scene.

Dan Jones and the Cut-Rate Liquor Store deny that
Watkins was intoxicated on the evening of April 5 when
he was in their store. Jones says that Watkins did not
appear to be intoxicated when he observed Watkins in the
store. Watkins was convicted of public intoxication at a
prior trial. Watkins is not present for this Cut-Rate case.

1. Prepare to do a direct examination of Officer Bier for
the government.

2. Prepare to do a cross examination of Officer Bier for
the Defense.

Officer Bier's Report

NITA LIQUOR COMMISSION OFFICIAL REPORT

My partner Donald Smith and I are investigators for the Nita Liquor Commission. On the evening of April 5, at approximately 8:45 p.m., we were parked near the Cut-Rate Liquor Store when we observed an individual, later identified as Walter Watkins, attempting to cross 7th Street. Mr. Watkins was staggering and had great difficulty making it to the other side of the street. He stumbled and almost fell at the curb on the south side of 7th Street. He walked to the entrance of the Cut-Rate Liquor Store, and then paused for a few moments before he entered the store. The front of the store had a plate glass window with displays and advertising in it. From our car, we could see Mr. Watkins from the shoulders up through the window. We observed Mr. Watkins approach the counter and say a few words to the clerk, Dan Jones. A few minutes later, Watkins emerged from the store carrying a bottle of Thunderbird wine in a brown paper sack.

I stopped Mr. Watkins as he exited the store. I detected the odor of alcohol and administered a field sobriety test. I then arrested Watkins and issued him a citation for public intoxication, seized the wine, and issued a citation to Dan Jones and the Cut-Rate Liquor store for violation of H.R.S. 281-78 which contains the following language:

> No licensee nor its employees shall sell or furnish any liquor to any person at the time under the influence of liquor.

I have attached a diagram of the scene to this report.

Date: April 5   Time: 22:15

signed J. Bier

_____

Diagram of Cut-Rate Liquor Store Area

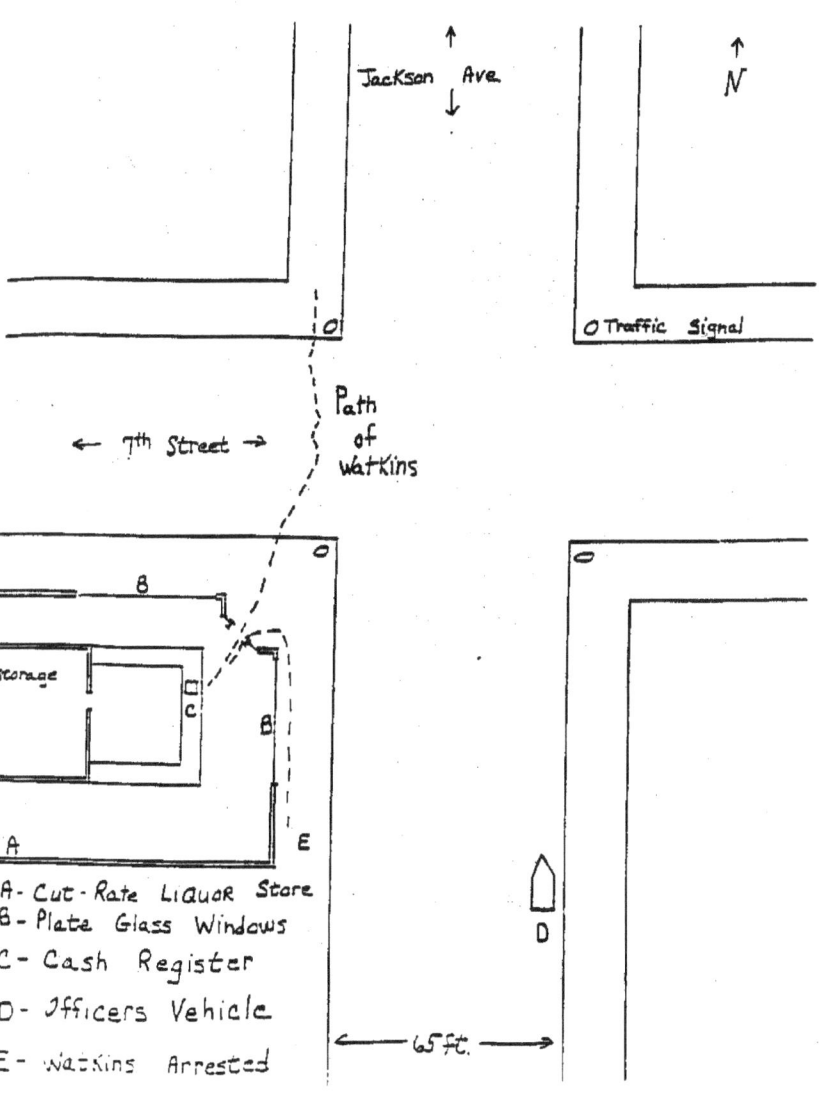

Photograph of a Scene

Introduce a photograph of Cut-Rate Liquor Store where the clerk and the liquor store were charged with selling liquor to an intoxicated person. FRE 901(B)(1) (Testimony of a Witness with Knowledge)

Q: Officer Bier, where were you on the night of April 5?
A: Parked in an unmark car outside Cut-Rate Liquor Store.

Q: Let me show you what has been marked as Plaintiff's proposed exhibit # 1. What is it?
A: It is a photograph of Cut-Rate Liquor Store where I was parked on April 5th.

Q: How do you know that?
A: I was at the store that night. I recognize it. I took the photo.

Q: Is the photograph a fair and accurate representation of Cut-Rate Liquor store as it appeared on April 5th?
A: Yes.

Q: Your Honor, I offer the exhibit into evidence.

Enhancements/Additional Questions
- "Please describe the appearance of the store."
- "How many times have you seen the Cut-Rate Liquor Store?" (Ask this question only if the witness has been to the store many times. However, being there once is enough for the foundation.) The witness can authenticate the photo even if the trial event was the only time the witness ever saw the store pictured in the photo

Additional Points:
- The photographer is not a necessary witness.
- The witness's personal knowledge of the contents of the photograph is all that is necessary.
- The witness does not have to have seen the photograph before coming to court.
- Print the photo and bring copies to court for the judge, jury, and opposing counsel.
- The photo could be a "Street view" from Google Maps that the witness has never seen before.

Diagram of the Scene

Demonstrative Evidence

Diagram from Officer Bier's Report

After some testimony about the events.

Q: Officer Bier, did you make a diagram of the scene that night? (Ans: Yes)

Q: Let me show you what has been marked as Plaintiff's proposed exhibit # 1. What is it? (Ans: My diagram)

Q: How do you know that? (Ans: I drew it. I remember it. That's my writing)

Q: Is it a fair and accurate representation of the intersection of Jackson and 7th Streets on April 5th? (Ans: Yes.)

Q: Is the proposed exhibit in the same condition as it was when you drew it on April 5th? (Ans: Yes.)

Q: Your Honor, I offer the exhibit into evidence.

Real Evidence

The Bottle of Thunderbird Wine Seized by Officer Bier

After some testimony about the events.

Q: Officer Bier, <u>what, if anything, did you recover</u> from Mr. Watkins that night?
(Ans: A bottle and a bag)

Q: Let me hand you what has been marked as Plaintiff's proposed exhibit # 2. <u>What is it?</u>
(Ans: The bottle and bag I seized from Watkins)

[If the bottle is in a bag, leave it in the bag. Have both the bottle and bag marked separately, e.g., Exhibits 1 and 2, A and B, 1 and 1A. Let the witness take the bottle out of the bag, like unwrapping a present. It will create some interest in what might be an otherwise boring trial.]

Q: <u>How do you know that?</u>
[Ans: My initials, in my handwriting, are on the bag along with the words "Cut-Rate Liquor" and "April 5."]

Q: Is the proposed exhibit # 2 <u>in the same or substantially the same condition</u> as it was when you recovered it from Watkins on April 5th?
(Ans: Generally, yes. However, some of the liquid was removed for testing for alcohol.)

Q: Your Honor, I offer the exhibit into evidence.

Offering A Contract into Evidence

Q: Mr. Johnny, I now want to ask you some questions about your dealings with Mr. King. In September, two years ago, did you have several conversations with Mr. King?

A: Yes. I did.

Q: What was the result of those conversations?

A: Mr. King and I entered into a contract for legal work.

Assume the exhibit has been pre-<u>marked</u> before the day of trial

Q: Let the record reflect that I am <u>handing</u> Mr. Johnny what has been pre-marked, as required by Court Rule, Plaintiff's proposed Exhibit # 1.
<u>What is it Mr. Johnny?</u>

A: It's the contract between me and Mr. King for the legal work that I was going to do for him.

Q: <u>How do you know that?</u> [Prepare the witness to answer this question]

A: I drafted this contract. I recognize it. That's my signature on it as well as Mr. King's.

Q: Is the contract in the <u>same condition</u> as it was two years when you both signed it.

A: Yes. There are no alterations to the contract.

Q: You Honor, I <u>offer </u>the exhibit into evidence

Refreshing Memory
(Anything can be used to refresh memory)

Refreshing memory is almost always done on direct examination.
Impeachment is almost always done on cross examination.

In the NITA case, assume witness Bier forgets some of Mr. Watkin's movements on the street. Refresh Bier's memory from his report. R612.

Q: Please describe Watkin's movements as he crossed 7th Street.
A: He staggered and had great difficulty getting to the other side of the street.

Q: Do you recall anything else about Watkins as he crossed the street.
A: Not really

Q: Officer Bier <u>did you make a report</u> in this case? A: Yes.

Q: Let me hand you what has been marked as Plaintiff's proposed exhibit # 3. <u>What is it?</u>
[Note: You are not going to introduce the document. Some judges might allow you to refresh memory without marking the exhibit, but the better practice is to have the document marked.]
A: My report.

Q: Please <u>read it to yourself</u>, especially the 4th and 5th lines.
(Note: You can focus the witness on what you want to witness to pay attention to.)

Q: <u>Let the record reflect that I am taking proposed exhibit # 3 away</u> from the Officer.
Now Officer Bier, is your memory refreshed?
A: Yes.

Q: What else do you now recall about how Watkins crossed 7th Street?
A: Watkins stumbled as he crossed 7th Street

(Discussion continued on the next page)

Recommendation: I suggest that you do not ask the witness, "Would anything refresh your memory." Just start refreshing. Isn't it strange to say, "Witness, I know you cannot remember, but can you remember anything that would help you remember what you have already forgotten?" Just refresh.

Additional points: The document used to refresh is not introduced into evidence. The witness' memory was refreshed. There is no need to introduce the document. There is no hearsay issue.

Writing Used to Refresh Memory

If a writing was used to refresh memory, R612 allows

as a matter of right, if the document was used in court;
with judge's discretion, if the document was used out of court

the opponent to:

1) see the writing in court,
2) inspect it
3) cross-examine on it, and
4) introduce portions of it (related to the testimony)

Simply: **Get (produced), Inspect, Cross, Introduce.**

However, it would be very unusual for an opponent to introduce the document because most of the document would hurt the opponent's case. If the opponent wanted to introduce only portions of the document, the lawyer who used it to refresh memory would have an argument that under R106, in fairness other parts of the document should be considered at the same time.

FRE 612. Writing used to refresh memory. (paraphrased)
 If a witness uses a writing to refresh memory for the purpose of testifying, either:
 (1) while testifying; or
 (2) before testifying, if the court in its discretion determines it is necessary in the interests of justice,
 an adverse party is entitled
 to have the writing produced at the hearing,
 to inspect it,
 to cross-examine the witness thereon, and
 to introduce in evidence those portions which relate to the
 testimony of the witness.

Refreshing Memory
with a Leading Question

(Using the same facts as the previous example)

Q: Do you recall anything else about Watkins as he crossed the street.

A: Not really

Q: Did he stumble and almost fall?

Opposing Lawyer: Objection: Leading

Q: I'll rephrase my question. What else do you recall about Watkins as he crossed the street.

A: Now I recall that he did stumble and almost fell crossing the street. I'm nervous. I forgot.

Note: The witness's credibility might have decreased somewhat because of the leading question, but the lawyer got the answer that was needed. The less important the information, the more likely leading will have little or no impact on your case.

Leading on Minor Issues
When the Witness Has Gone Off Course

Q: What day of the week did this happen?

A: Tuesday.

Q: You said Tuesday. Did you actually mean Monday?

A: Oh right, sorry. It was Monday.

Recorded Recollection (Author's Rule)

Recorded recollection is a hearsay exception that allows <u>for reading into evidence</u> a statement that was made by a witness on the stand who can no longer recall the facts even after there has been attempts to refresh the witness's memory. Recorded recollection is <u>almost always done on direct examination</u> with a witness the lawyer has called to testify. This foundation is complicated and not intuitive.

In the NITA problem, assume that attempts to refresh the witness's memory did not work. Therefore, assume the previous question and answer were:

Q: What else do you now recall?
A: Sorry, I truly do not remember any more.

[Lawyer now moves into the foundation for Recorded Recollection, under R803(5).

Q: Let me again show you proposed exhibit # 3. That is your report of this incident, right? (Note: Leading is appropriate when establishing any foundations under FRE 104(a) and similar state rules).
A: Yes

Q: You made that report when the incident was <u>fresh</u> in your mind?
A: Yes, just about an hour after the incident.

Q: Does the report <u>accurately reflect your knowledge</u> of the incident at the time of the incident?
A: Yes.

Q: Although you <u>once knew the details</u> of the incident and wrote them in your report, right now <u>you cannot now recall</u> the details of the incident well enough <u>to testify fully and accurately</u>, right?
A: Yes.

Q: Your honor, I would now <u>like to read</u> into the record those parts of the report that the witness no longer remembers. [Or, you could ask to have the witness read the portions of the report.]

(Discussion continued on the next page)

FRE 803(5) Recorded Recollection A record that:

(A) is on a matter the witness once knew about but now cannot recall well enough to testify fully and accurately;

(B) was made or adopted by the witness when the matter was fresh in the witness's memory; and

(C) accurately reflects the witness's knowledge.

If admitted, the record may be read into evidence but may be received as an exhibit only if offered by an adverse party.

Additional Points: "Admission" into evidence comes from reading parts of the document into evidence. The document is <u>not physically admitted</u> by the proponent of the evidence. It cannot be taken into the jury room. Information in this hearsay document is admitted (heard) only once like oral testimony. Also, admitting information from a "Learned Treatise" under that hearsay exception R803(18) is a similar process in that the information from the treatise can only be read and not physically introduced.

Almost always, the witness was the author of the document used as the recorded recollection. Refreshing memory under R612 and recorded recollection are almost always done on direct examination. Witnesses are impeached on cross, not refreshed. You would not normally use recorded recollection on cross because almost all of the document goes against your client.

I think <u>most lawyers prefer to read the recollection on direct examination themselves</u> and not have the witness read it. By reading the recollection yourself, you can add what you consider the best tone, volume, pace, and emphasis for your case. Remember, when you use a past recollection recorded with your witness on direct, you cannot physically introduce the document into evidence. The proponent of the past recollection recorded "admits" the recollection by reading it, not physically admitting it.

<u>Recorded recollection documents are not business records. Business records do get admitted into evidence</u>. The difference is that if admitted, the evidence can be taken into the jury room and be consulted by the jury many times during deliberations.

A past recollection recorded includes all notes that a witness makes on any type of document. In evidence class, I pull out my wallet and show students all the recorded recollections that I have in my wallet (post-it notes, notes on business cards, notes on little scraps of paper, etc.) and any notes I have taken on my cell phone. Recorded Recollections and Statements in Learned Treatises under R803(18) are two types of hearsay documents which can only be read into evidence but not physically introduced, at least not by the proponent of a recorded recollection.

Business Records - Custodian of Records
(The actual hearsay exception is for "Regularly Conducted Activity," but is usually called "Business Records")

To prove that Cut-Rate Liquors had Thunderbird Wine in stock on April 5, a business record can be offered.

Q: Please state your name, occupation, and why you are here today.

A: I am Mr. Data, an employee of Cut-Rate Liquors. My duties at Cut-Rate include serving as the custodian of business inventory records for Cut-Rate. I am here today pursuant to a subpoena to bring inventory records of Cut-Rate for April 5th.

Q: Did you bring with you today a copy of the Cut-Rate inventory records pertaining to Thunderbird wine for April 5th with you?

A: Yes.

Q: Do you know how Cut-Rate maintains its inventory records?

A: Yes.

Q: I show you what has been pre-marked as proposed exhibit # 1 and ask if you can identify what it is?

A: Yes, I can. Those are the Cute-Rate inventory records that I brought to court.

Q: Are those inventory records made by a person with <u>personal knowledge,</u> <u>at or near the time</u> the inventory is taken?

A: Yes.

Q: Are those records <u>kept in the course of a regularly conducted activity</u> of a business?

A: Yes.

Q: Is making those records a <u>regular practice</u> of Cut-Rate's business?

A: Yes.

Q: Your Honor, I offer the exhibit into evidence.

Publishing a Business Record: After being admitted, the business record can be "published" (which means it can be shown to the trier to fact). Depending on the judge's practice, the lawyer might be able to have the information from the record read to jury when it is admitted. If so, the Q & A could be:

Q: What do those records say about whether Cut-Rate had Thunderbird Wine in stock on April 5th?
A: "Thunderbird Wine, quantity 5," which means that Cut-Rate had five bottles of Thunderbird Wine in stock on April 5.

Remember, **business records are KRAP**. That acronym always gets my students' attention, and it helps them remember the foundation's components. **KRAP** – means:
Kept in the course,
Regular practice,
At or near the time,
Personal knowledge

The **custodian of records or other qualified witness** required by the business record evidence rule is often the owner of the business, a bookkeeper, or anybody who works in the business. They just have to be able to answer questions to provide the appropriate foundation.

Although it adds to the weight of the evidence to have a witness who has been employed for many years in the data collection of the business, that is not required. The custodian only needs to be able to testify to the foundation requirements. The custodian could have only been the custodian for one day, if they can credibly answer the foundational questions (although that fact might go to the weight of the evidence, but not its admissibility). The custodian does not have to be employed on the day the record was made.

I would prefer to use a self-authenticating business record. The custodian is open to a difficult cross.
"Do you know who made the business entry?" – Know their work history? Have they been disciplined? Know their accuracy? Are they still with the company? (Of course, you need a good faith basis to ask such cross questions).

Self-Authenticating Business Records

The Federal Rules of Evidence were amended in 2002 to allow business records to be self-authenticated by a written certification of the custodian or other qualified witness, which means that a witness does not have to appear in court. FRE 902(11)(12). Many states have created statutes or forms to be used for the certification. An example of such a certification affidavit follows and many are available on the internet.

> 32 of the 50 U.S. states have rules on self-authenticating business
> records (records of regularly conducted activity)

Texas Form – A Sample

	Business Records Affidavit	
FORM AR-1(05/10)	Tax Year	HCAD Account Number

This affidavit should be executed before a Notary Public or other official authorized to administer oaths and attached to the applicable business records. Please print or type.

Before me, the undersigned authority, personally appeared _____, who being by me duly sworn, deposed as follows:

My name is _____, I am of sound mind, capable of making this affidavit, and personally acquainted with the facts herein stated:

I am the custodian of the records of _____ Attached hereto are
(NAME OF BUSINESS)
_____ pages of records from _____. These
(NAME OF BUSINESS)
said _____ pages of records are kept by _____
(NAME OF BUSINESS)
in the regular course of business, and it was the regular practice of said entity for an employee or representative with knowledge of the act, event, condition, opinion, or diagnosis, recorded to make the record or to transmit information thereof to be included in such record; and the record was made at or near the time or reasonably soon thereafter. The records attached hereto are the original or exact duplicates of the original.

_____
Affiant's Signature

SWORN TO AND SUBSCRIBED before me on the _____ day of _____, _____.

_____
Notary Public, State of Texas

(seal)

_____
Notary's Printed Name

_____
My commission expires

Demonstrative Evidence
Similar to the Real Item

Assume the bottle of Thunderbird wine in the Nita Liquor Commission case was dropped and broken after the contents had been tested in the lab and showed that it contained alcohol. At trial, a lawyer wants to introduce a bottle similar to the actual bottle of Thunderbird wine.

Q: Officer Bier, do you recognize proposed exhibit # 5?
A: Yes. I do.

Q: What is it?
A: It is a bottle like the one sold by Cut-Rate on the night of the incident.

Q: How do you know that?
A: I am a Liquor Commission Investigator. I am very familiar with Thunderbird wine as part of my job.

Q: "Is this bottle similar to the bottle you seized from Watkins on April 5?"
A: Yes.

Q: I offer the exhibit into evidence.

If there is a relevance objection to the "similar" bottle, the lawyer examining the witness needs to be ready to say, "Your honor, this bottle is relevant to show ...[some appropriate statement]." For example, the size and weight of the bottle suggests that Mr. Watkins could not have smuggled the bottle into the liquor store under his clothing. The similar bottle is not offered as the bottle that was sold that night, but it is being offered to prove something else, which is an example of limited admissibility under FRE 105. The lawyer should not say, although it might be true, "My evidence professor always told us to introduce some physical evidence into the trial to wake up the trier of fact." [Such a statement offers a good trial strategy, but not a good response to the judge's question about relevance.]

Impeachment by Prior Written Inconsistent Statement
FRE 613

Impeach Officer Bier from his report in the NITA problem, assuming Bier testified on direct exam, "I saw Watkins from the waist up inside the store."

> Direct exam testimony was "...from the waist up...."
> Report says "...from the shoulders up..."

Q: Today you testified on direct examination[1] that you could see Watkins inside the store from the waist up? (said in a disbelieving tone) (Commit to today's testimony.)

A: Yes.

Q: You made a written report in this case within a few hours of the incident? (Credit prior statement's reliability)

A: Yes.

Q: Let the record reflect that I am handing the witness proposed exhibit #x. Mr. Bier, proposed exhibit #x is the report you made within a couple of hours after the incident?

A: Yes.

Q: That is your signature on the report?

A: Yes

Q: Even though you said on direct examination that you could see Mr. Watkins inside the store from the waist up, doesn't it say right here in your report (pointing to it) that "we could see Mr. Watkins from the shoulders up through the window"?

A: Yes.

---

[1] I suggest that you only use the phrase – "You testified on direct" – when you are going to impeach a witness with a prior statement. Do not use that phrase when you are asking questions about a real event that took place in your case. What happened on the day of the incident might be different that what a witness testified to on direct. You should keep the trier of fact's attention on the incident itself, not the testimony on direct – unless you are impeaching that direct testimony.

(Discussion continued on the next page)
Stop. Ask no further questions on this topic. Don't say, "Are you lying today or were you lying then?" Such a question is probably argumentative and objectionable anyway. Do not argue with the witness or ask the witness to admit they are not telling the truth. Save the credibility argument for closing argument. In closing argument, you can make an argument without having the witness trying to explain away your impeachment.

Understand the difference between testimony about "waist up" and "shoulders up." If Officer Bier could see Mr. Watkins inside the store from the waist up, he could have seen the bottle of wine, the cash register, any money changing hands, and the wine bottle changing hands. All those facts go to showing that there was a sale of wine in violation of the statute. However, if the officer could only see inside the store at the shoulders up level, then he was not able to see any direct sale and the defense has a better argument.

Three impeaching steps here: commit; credit; and confront. 1) Commit the witness to the statement made on direct, 2) credit the prior out-of-court statement, and 3) confront the witness with the difference.

By putting the conflicting statements in one sentence by using a dependent clause ("Even though you said on direct examination that…"), the trier of fact cannot miss the contradiction. Some impeaching lawyers will emphasize certain words in their questions, so the trier of fact does not miss the inconsistency. For example, they would emphasize with tone, volume, pace, and any other nonverbal's, the words "waist up" and "shoulder up." The impeaching lawyer might want to make eye contact with the judge or the jury when emphasizing those words.

Additional questions that are sometimes asked, especially if it is a jury trial:
> Your prior statement was made closer in time to the event than your statement today?
> Your memory was better at the earlier time?
> You have had training on how to write reports?

You know that your supervisor will read your reports?
You know that you are evaluated on, and perhaps even promoted
or demoted based on the quality of your reports?

Impeachment by Omission

Assume that <u>Bier testified on direct exam</u>, "As I was sitting in
my car watching Watkins <u>inside the store, I saw that Watkins</u>
<u>stumble and almost fall as he approached the counter.</u>" However,
Officer Bier's report does not say that Watkins stumbled and
almost fell inside the store. In fact, the report indicates that the
officer could only see Watkins from the shoulders up as he
approached the counter. Impeachment by omission - meaning that
the witness testified in court to something that was not in the report
- it is a little harder to accomplish than a direct prior inconsistent
statement, but it is still very doable.

Q: <u>You testified on direct</u> examination that you saw Mr.
       Watkins stumble and almost fall as he approached the
       counter inside from the store? (Credit prior statement's
       reliability)
A: Yes.

Q: You made a written report in this case within an hour of the
       incident, right?
A: Yes.

Q: I am handing the witness proposed exhibit #x.
       This is the report you made within a couple of hours after the
       incident, isn't it?
A: Yes.

Q: That is your signature on the report, isn't that true?
A: Yes

Q: <u>Even though you said on direct examination</u> that you saw Mr.
       Watkins <u>stumble and almost fall</u> as he approached the
       counter <u>inside</u> the store, <u>nowhere</u> in this report that you
       prepared <u>does it state</u> that you saw Watkins stumble and
       almost fall <u>inside</u> the store, does it? [If the witness takes time

to look for it in the report, give them as much time as they want to take.

A: No, it doesn't say that.

The report says nothing about Watkins' behavior in the store. Behavior in the store is critical to proving that defendant Jones knew that Watkins was intoxicated.

Additional questions beyond the bare-bones foundation.
    Lawyer could build up the report, for example:

> "You try to put everything that is important in the report, right?"
> "They taught you to do that in the department training, right?"

The potential re-direct examination:
If it were my witness who was impeached, my redirect would go something like this:
    Q: Officer, how do you explain what seems to be an inconsistency between your direct testimony that Watkins stumbled inside the store and your report, which does not mention Watkins stumbled inside the store?
    A: [Perhaps the best answer would be] I can't put everything into the report. But I clearly remember that he stumbled inside the store.

Impeachment by Inconsistent Oral Deposition

Assume the same factual inconsistency of testimony on direct examination that Mr. Watkins stumbled inside the store, but this time also assume that Officer Bier gave an oral deposition under oath and gave an answer that did not mention any stumbling inside the store.

After laying a foundation which would include the procedures involved in the deposition, such as:
- You came to my office?
- You took an oath to tell the truth?
- I told you that if you didn't understand the question, you should tell me you don't understand?
- You had an opportunity to review and correct the transcript some weeks after the deposition?
- After you read the typed deposition, you signed the deposition as being accurate?

then complete the impeachment by reading the questions that were asked and the answers that were given at the deposition.

The impeaching sequence could go something like this:

Q: Even though you said on direct that Watkins stumbled and almost fell in the store when he was at the counter, at your deposition weren't you asked this question, and didn't you give this answer:

> Q: Now Officer Bier, how was Watkins walking when he was inside the store?
> A: I can't say for sure. My view into the store was obstructed.

A: Yes, that is what it says.

You want to confine your questions to what the witness said at the deposition, not what the witness remembers now. Your opponent will no doubt do redirect examination to try to rehabilitate the witness.

Impeachment by Inconsistent Oral Deposition - **Short Form**

On direct examination, the witness said, "The light was <u>green</u>."

You want to impeach with the witness' deposition that says, "The light was <u>red</u>."

Q: On direct examination you said the light was green?
A: Yes.

Q: Even though on direct examination you said that the light was green, at the deposition weren't you asked the following question, and didn't you give the following answer?
Q: What color was the light?
A: The light was red.
A: Yes.

Impeachment by Inconsistent Oral Deposition - Long Form

On direct examination, the witness said, "The light was green."
You want to impeach with the witness' deposition that says,
"The light was red."

Highlight the inconsistency
Q. On direct examination you said the light was green. [A: Yes]
Q. There is no question in your mind about that? [A: No question.]

Lock the witness into the testimony (you can omit this step)
Q. Have you ever said anything different? [No]
Q. Are you sure it was green? [Yes]
Q. Isn't it true that the light was in fact red? [No]

Build up the impeaching document
Q. You remember coming to my office to answer some questions?
Q. You came for a deposition on July 11, last year?
Q. I asked you questions, and you gave me answers, isn't that right?
Q. Your lawyer sat next to you while you answered?
Q. A court reporter took down your answers?
Q. That reporter gave you an oath to tell the truth?
Q. You agreed to tell the truth?
Q. After that deposition, the Q's and A's were typed up and you
   had a chance to read them over?
Q. After making sure it was correct, you signed it didn't you?
Q. This is your signature, isn't it?
Q. This deposition was just four months after the accident?
Q. Even though on direct examination you said that the light was
   green, at the deposition weren't you asked the following
   question, and didn't you give the following answer?
   Q: What color was the light?
   A: The light was red.

Impeachment by Inconsistent Oral Statement
(Assuming only the cross-examining lawyer heard the inconsistent statement)

Assume that although Bier testified on direct exam that "Watkins stumbled and almost fell inside the store," Bier was overheard outside the courtroom say to a person who is not available to testify, "I never really saw Watkins stumble inside the store." However, only the lawyer for Cut-Rate Liquor heard Bier's statement.

This is an inconsistent oral statement. Unlike most inconsistent statements, this one was <u>not made prior</u> to the in-court testimony on direct exam. <u>This statement was made after</u> the in-court testimony.

This fact pattern presents a special problem if the lawyer was the only person who overhead the statement. If Bier denies making the statement, the cross-examiner does not have a witness who could be called to the stand to complete the impeachment of Bier. So, if no one other that the lawyer overhead the statement, what can the lawyer do? Although no evidence rule prohibits the lawyer from testifying, rules of professional conduct in most jurisdictions would prohibit prevent the lawyer from testifying. What can the lawyer do?

Probably the best solution would be for the impeaching lawyer to be as detailed as possible during the cross leading up to the impeaching question. If the trier of fact believes the details, the trier of fact might believe that Bier also made the final statement ("I never saw him stumble inside the store.").

The detailed cross could do something like this.
Q: During the break, you went outside the courtroom, right?
Q: And you sat on the bench outside?
Q: You sat next to a man wearing a blue shirt, right?
Q: And the two of you had a conversation?
Q: You talked for about 5 minutes, right?
Q: "Even though you said on direct exam in court just 30 minutes ago that Watkins stumbled and almost fell in the store when he was at the counter, didn't you say to a man on a bench outside this courtroom just 10 minutes ago, "I never really saw Watkins stumble inside the store?"

Using Learned Treatises

**FRE 803. Exceptions to the Rule Against Hearsay —
Regardless of Whether the Declarant Is Available as a Witness**
The following are not excluded by the rule against hearsay,
regardless of whether the declarant is available as a witness:
**(18) Statements in Learned Treatises, Periodicals, or
Pamphlets.** A statement contained in a treatise, periodical, or
pamphlet if:

    (A) the statement is <u>called to the attention of an expert</u> witness
    on cross-examination or relied on by the expert on direct
    examination; and

    (B) the publication is established as a <u>reliable authority</u> by the
    expert's admission or testimony, by another expert's testimony,
    or by judicial notice.

If admitted, the statement may be <u>read</u> into evidence <u>but not
received</u> as an exhibit.

**Perspective: 38 of the 50 states have a similar or identical
rule;**
7 state rules only allow use of the treatise for impeachment
(California, Florida, Georgia, Michigan, Oregon, Tennessee, and
Virginia); 5 states have no rule (Illinois, Massachusetts,
Missouri, New York, and Pennsylvania).

---

3 Key Points for Using the Learned Treatise

**To use a learned treatise on either direct or cross-examination,
under FRE 803(18)**
1) there must be an expert <u>on the witness stand,</u>
2) the treatise has been established as a <u>reliable authority</u>, and
3) the statement may be <u>only read</u> into the record, but the treatise
cannot be physically introduced into evidence.

Learned Treatises:
Use on Direct Exam to Support Your Expert
FRE 803(18) – Hearsay Exception

After an expert testifies that it is not possible to determine if the plaintiff's epileptic seizures are caused by the plaintiff's auto accident, the following questioning takes place to use a learned treatise to support the expert's opinion. This is an example of using a "paper expert," or said another way, getting the opinion of two experts but only calling one as a witness.

Q: Dr. Rosenberg, are you familiar with the text called Medicine written by Dr. Mark Fishman?

A: Yes

Q: Let me show you proposed exhibit #1. What is it?

A: It is the book called Medicine written by Dr. Mark Fishman.

Q: Is it a recognized as a reliable authority in the field of medicine?

A: Yes

Q: What does the Fishman text say about the causes of epileptic seizures?

A: On page 135, Fishman says that a cause is found for seizures in less than 25% of the cases.

Using a learned treatise as a hearsay exception can only done by reading the treatise to the trier of fact, but not by physically introducing the treatise into evidence. FRE 803(18)

Learned Treatises: Use on Cross to Attack the Opposing Expert FRE 803(18) – Hearsay Exception

After establishing that Mark Fishman's text called "Medicine" is a reliable authority in the field of medicine, either by your expert, or by your opponent's expert, or by judicial notice (Note: judges seldom take such judicial notice), the lawyer below uses the learned treatise on cross examination to contradict the opposing party's expert witness. A statement in a treatise can be used to impeach the opponent's expert and as substantive evidence (meaning for the truth of the statement – this is a hearsay exception).

Q: Dr. Barron, you testified during your direct examination that Mr. Fulbright's epilepsy was caused by the auto accident, right?
A: Yes.

Q: Dr., there is no medical evidence that Mr. Fulbright showed any clinical evidence of brain injury immediately after the incident is there?
A: That's correct.

Q: And no evidence of a skull fracture?
A: That's also correct.

Q: And no evidence of bloody spinal fluid, right?
A: Correct again.

Q: Dr., doesn't the text called, Medicine, written by Mark Fishman, indicate on page 132 that the four symptoms most commonly found with epileptic seizures are 1) loss of consciousness, 2) clinical evidence of brain injury immediately after the incident, 3) skull fracture, and 4) bloody spinal fluid?
A: Yeah, Fishman does say that.

Q: Your Honor, no further questions.

Voicemail, Phone Conversations, Recorded Phone Conversations

There is nothing special about the identification of a telephone call. Authentication for voice identification is covered in FRE 901(b)(5)&(6).

Do you know X?

How do you know X?

How long have you known X?

Have you ever spoken with X on the phone?

How often have you spoken with X on the phone?

On [the day in question] did you have a phone conversation with X?

Who initiated that call?

[If **your** witness initiated the call]

> How did you make the call? [Ans: used contacts list on my cell phone; used recent call list on cell phone; used landline]
>
> Was their name already in your cell phone from previous calls to them?
>
> Did you recognize the voice when your call was answered?
>
> Who were you talking to?

(Continued on next page)

[If the **other party** initiated the call]

Could you tell who was calling you?

How could you tell who was calling you? [Name appeared on my cell phone]

Why did their name appear in your cell phone? [I had name in my contacts list from many previous calls]

Who was on the phone when you answered the call? [The defendant]

How did you know that? [We have talked many times before. I recognized his voice.]

What did he say during that call?

Digital Evidence
Electronically Stored Information – ESI

Electronically Stored Information (EIS) includes emails, text messages, websites, fax, social media, computer printouts, and other digital records. Although evidence professors will tell you that the classic rules of evidence, created long before cell phones, computers, and the Internet, are more than adequate for the new digital world, some people may doubt it.

Yet truly, introducing digital evidence in court still does apply the same basic "HARROWing" principles found in all evidence codes – whether introducing physical items or digital evidence.

"HARROWing" is my pneumonic to remind us of evidence principles to consider when introducing physical pieces of evidence, especially physical evidence with words on or in it. HARROWing - defined as extremely distressing, agonizing, excruciating, torturing, painful, and causing physical or psychological pain – is how many new lawyers describe their experience trying to introduce evidence

H = Hearsay; FRE 800s
A= Authentication; FRE 900s
R= FRE R401 relevancy (sometime called "logical relevancy);
R= FRE403 (sometimes called "legal Relevancy);
OW = FRE 1000s Original Writings (traditionally known as Best Evidence).

The same rules of evidence apply to ESI as they do to paper and physical evidence. The most challenging foundational issues for digital evidence are establishing:1) who created the digital evidence (the author), and 2) has it been altered?

A Variety of Standards

Different standards have developed in various U.S. state for authenticating digital evidence. The law is still developing.

The Texas courts, and probably most jurisdictions, use an authentication standard identical to the standard used for traditional forms of evidence – "evidence sufficient to support a finding (FRE 901). The Texas standard can be thought of and remembered by the state's placement on a map – it is a lower standard.

However, the Maryland courts, and a few others, have developed a higher standard – like Maryland's placement on a map. Maryland courts seem to require that the proponent of digital evidence prove that the digital evidence has not been altered or hacked, it comes from a certain source, and that no one other than the owner could have used the electronic device to send or post the message. This view of EIS authentication is concerned about "voodoo information taken from the Internet." It creates a standard that can seldom be met.

The Grimm, Joseph & Capra article, Best Practices for Authenticating Digital Evidence 69 Baylor L.R. 1 (2017) is a great source for understanding factors in authenticating digital evidence. That article presents an overview of how FRE 104(a) and 104(b) interact in the authentication process and the article argues that digital evidence should be authenticated requiring only evidence

"sufficient to support a finding," - which is a low standard.

The authors offer the opinion that,

"Generally speaking, it will be a rare case in which an item of digital evidence cannot be authenticated."

The article covers various ways to authenticate digital evidence. Most helpful will be the examples of various types of circumstantial evidence that would qualify as "distinctive characteristics" under FRE 901(b)(4). Additional, less frequently used methods of authenticating evidence are also covered, such as, personal knowledge of a witness, business records (in some email situations), jury comparison, and production in discovery.

Distinctive Characteristics and Circumstantial Evidence Used to Authenticate Emails and Text Messages as Having Been Sent by A Particular Person Or As Having Been Received by A Particular Person

There are many possible ways to use circumstantial evidence to qualify as "distinctive characteristics" to authenticate Electronically Stored Information (ESI) under FRE 901(b)(4) Distinctive Characteristics and the Like. Appearance, contents, substance, internal patterns, or other distinctive characteristics of the item taken together with all the circumstances are almost endless.

The Grimm, Joseph & Capra article offers many extremely valuable suggestions about circumstantial evidence which can be considered "distinctive characteristics" and used to authenticate digital evidence under R901(b)(4).

For example, when laying the foundation for an email or text, consider:
1) information in or about the email or text
2) information outside the email or text itself that leads back to the author
3) forensic information, and
4) information outside the email or text itself indicating receipt of the message.

Factors suggested by Grimm, Joseph, and Capra used to authenticate authorship or receipt of a message include:

1) information in or about the email or text, such as:
- the email address, email signature, a nickname, a screen name, initials, a moniker, the author's customary use of emoji or emoticons, a writing style (including phrases and abbreviations frequently used by the author), referring to facts only the author or small group of people would know about, facts uniquely tied to the author, information about the author's family, photos of the author, items of

importance to the author such as a car or a pet, and other such information

2) information outside the email or text itself that leads back to the author, such as:
- the email was part of a chain or series of emails from the same person, the claimed author told the witness to expect an email from the author, the author orally repeats its content soon after the email is sent, the author discusses the contents of the email with the third party, the author leaves a voicemail substantially of the same content, and other such information

3) forensic information, such as:
- an email's hash values or testimony from a forensic witness that the email came from a particular device at a particular time, and other such information

4) information outside the email or text itself indicating receipt of the message, such as:
- a reply was received by the sender that came from the recipient, later conduct of the recipient reflects knowledge of the contents of the sent message, later communication of the recipient reflects knowledge of the message, and the message was received and accessed on an electronic device in the possession of the recipient, and other such information.

Presenting the Digital Evidence from a Cell Phone in Court

- Print the page from the phone and use the printout in court.
- If a photo comes from a cell phone, attach the picture to an email, and then print the picture from a computer.
- Screenshot the information (picture, text message, email, social media post), email it, then print from a computer.

Self-Authentication for Digital Evidence

Recent amendments to the Federal Rules of Evidence allow for self-authentication of certified records
– See FRE 902(11)(13)(14)

Digital Evidence and Self-Authentication

FRE 902 Self-authentication
(11) Certified Domestic Records of a Regularly Conducted Activity. The original or a copy of a domestic record that meets the requirements of FRE 803(6)(A)-(C), as shown by a <u>certification</u> of the custodian or another qualified person that complies with a federal statute or a rule prescribed by the Supreme Court. Before the trial or hearing, the proponent must give an adverse party <u>reasonable written notice</u> of the intent to offer the record — and must make the record and certification available for inspection — so that the party has a fair opportunity to challenge them.

> 39 states have similar or identical rules. Many states have created forms for self-authentication of business records.

FRE 902(13) (Added to FRE Dec. 2017)
(13) Certified Records Generated by an Electronic Process or System. A record generated by an electronic process or system that produces an accurate result, as shown by a <u>certification of a qualified person that complies with the certification requirements of FRE 902(11) or (12).</u> The proponent must also meet the notice requirements of FRE 902(11).
[This rule covers text messages, cell phone photos, GPS data, and other ESI]

> The following 9 states have this rule:
> Alabama, Arizona, Illinois, Mississippi, North Dakota, Ohio, Pennsylvania, Utah, and Wyoming.

FRE 902(14) Certified Data Copied from an Electronic Device, Storage Medium, or File. Data copied from an electronic device, storage medium, or file, if authenticated by a process of digital identification, as shown by a <u>certification of a qualified person that complies with the certification requirements of FRE 902(11) or (12)</u>. The proponent also must meet the notice requirements of FRE 902(11).

> The following 9 states have this rule:
> Alabama, Arizona, Illinois, Mississippi, North Dakota, Ohio, Pennsylvania, Utah, and Wyoming.

Email – Witness is the Sender (Outgoing Email)

Q: How did you notify Cut-Rate about …
A: I sent an email to Dan Jones

Q: What email address did you use?
A: DJones@Cutrate.com

Q: How do you know that was the correct address?
A: He and I have email back and forth for a few months, and all of his emails to me came from that email address

Q: Let me show you what has been marked as plaintiff's proposed exhibit #1.

Q: What is it? (A printout of the email I sent to Jones that day.).

Q: How do you know that? (I wrote it. I remember it. It was in my "sent mail" folder.)

Q: Your Honor I offer the exhibit into evidence.

Email – Witness is the Recipient (Incoming Email)

Do you know Dan Jones?

How do you know him?

Are you familiar with the email address DJones@Cutrate.com?

Have you received emails from Dan Jones in the past?

Have you sent emails to Dan Jones at that address?

Has he responded to your emails from that email address?

Is that email address in your email contacts?

In late April, did you receive an email from Dan Jones about selling liquor?

Did you recognize email address as being from Dan Jones?

I am handing you what has been marked as proposed exhibit #7. Do you recognize it?

What is it? (A: The email from Dan Jones)

Why would you say that's an email from Dan Jones?
[provide information about distinctive characteristics of this email]

How did you get a paper copy of this email? (A: I printed it out.)

Is this a true and accurate printout of that email?

Your Honor, I offer the proposed exhibit into evidence.

> [The email reads: "I might be getting fired. They caught me selling booze to drunks again."]

Text Message

Received by Witness

Do you know Y?

Do you communicate with Y on a regular basis?

In what ways to you communicate with Y?

Did you receive a text message from the Y [recently; on or about _ date, on the topic of ..., etc.]?

Would you recognize a printout of the message if you were to see it again?

Let me show you what has been marked as proposed exhibit # 1. Do you recognize it?

What is it? [Ans: A screenshot from my cell phone]

How do you know that this is a message from Y? [It is similar to other messages I have received from Y in that ...]

How did it appear when it arrived on your phone? [Showed up under the name and with the picture I had previously assigned to Y]

What other distinctive characteristics did you notice about the message? [provide as many as distinctive characteristics possible]

Is it a fair and accurate representation of the text message you received [recently; on or about _ date, on the topic of visiting your son, etc.]?

Has it been altered in any way?

I would like to enter the proposed exhibit into evidence

Social Media
Facebook, Instagram, Snapchat, Twitter, and other Posts

Do you know B?

How long have you known him?

Are you familiar with Facebook?

Does B have a Facebook account?

Have you seen posts by B on his Facebook account in the past?

How do you know that B made those posts? [provide distinctive characteristics]

Have you seen a posting on B's Facebook account about [the matter in question]?

Let the record reflect that I am handing you what has been marked as proposed exhibit 12 and ask if you can identify it?

What is it?

Is that a screenshot of the Facebook posting by B about ___?

What day did you take the screenshot?

Is it a true and accurate screenshot of that posting?

Is the post still on B's account? [Ask this question only if it is currently on the account.]

I offer the proposed exhibit into evidence.

Internet Website – Web Posting

Did you visit Professor John Barkai's webpage? [Yes]

How did you access it? [Googled "John Barkai" on my phone]

How did you find his page?
    Ans: "Yes, I clicked on the link that said
       "Prof. John Barkai Homepage.""

What did you find when you clicked on that link for the homepage?
    Ans: I found his list of courses and other posts.

Did you click on any particular link?
    Ans: I clicked Hawaii Rules of Evidence (HRE) Book Page

What did you find on that page when you clicked on it?
    A: I found a link to buy from Amazon a copy of several different evidence handbooks.

Let me show you what's been marked as proposed exhibit # 14.
    Can you identify it?
       A: Yes. It's a screenshot of that webpage with instructions about how to buy books from Amazon.

Was that screenshot a print of the page from his website?
       A: Yes, I printed it myself.

Is this exhibit a fair and accurate copy of that webpage?   [Yes]

Has this exhibit of the screenshot been altered or otherwise change from the image on your phone in any way?   [No]

I offer the exhibit into evidence.

Fax – Incoming

Does your office have a fax machine?

Do you send outgoing faxes?

Do you receive incoming faxes?

Have you received purchase orders from the defendant by fax in the past?

Let me show you plaintiff's proposed exhibit # 27 and ask if you can identify it? [A: Yes. I can]

What is it? [A: A fax I received about six months ago from the defendant]

Why do you say this fax came from the defendant?
A: There are number of factors in addition to the document being written on the defendant's letterhead stationery. The fax is signed by the head of defendant's purchasing department, and I am familiar with her signature from our past dealings. Further, imprinted on the bottom of this fax sheet is the fax number for the defendant's company, and I have faxed prior documents to the defendant by using that number. Finally, the document relates to the purchase of some equipment that I had discussed with the defendant's head of purchasing just a few hours before the fax arrived at my office.

Is this document in the same or substantially the same condition as it was when you received it?   [A: Yes, it is exactly the same.]

There have been no alterations or changes? [A: None whatsoever.]

Your Honor, I move that this proposed exhibit be admitted into evidence.

Expert Opinions

Admissibility of Expert Testimony.
The majority of U.S. states have explicitly adopted the Daubert (FRE702) standard for expert witness testimony
A minority of states use either the Frye ("general acceptance") standard or some combination of Daubert and Frye standards. Additionally, "general acceptance" is part of the Daubert standard.

Four Part Expert Opinion Foundation and Testimony

1. Elicit the background and qualifications of the expert
2. Tender or offer the witness as expert in a particular field (e.g., 'general medicine.")
   – Opponent is allowed to voir dire (test qualifications by cross examination limited to the expert's qualifications, but not the facts of this case)
3. Offer the expert's opinion or conclusion (to a particular standard such as "reasonable medical certainty") FRE 702
4. Offer the basis for opinion FRE703
   – Including reasonable reliance on inadmissible evidence
   – Disclosure of inadmissible evidence?

Three Simple Questions

1) Q: "Do you have an opinion as to whether…

2) Q: "What is that opinion?"

3) Q: "How did you reach that opinion?
   A: [including inadmissible information reasonably relied upon by experts in the particular field, FRE 703]

How to Start
The expert witness examination normally starts with questions to establish the witness' qualifications to testify as an expert.

Topics for Background and Qualifications of an Expert:
- formal education, work experience, number of previous times retained, qualified, and testified as an expert, in which courts, on-the-job training, non-degree training courses, publications in the field, teaching in the field, memberships in related professional associations, and any other topics relevant to showing the person is an expert.

Tender / Offer

After presenting the expert's background and qualifications, in jurisdictions where the judge must "certify" or "find" that the witness is an expert and is permitted to testify as an expert, the lawyer presenting the expert then "tenders" or "offers" the witness to the judge as an expert, stating the field of expertise.

"I offer/tender Mr. X as an expert in the field of…"

"I ask the court to certify Ms. Y as an expert in the field of …"

Can you call the expert an "expert?"

After any voir dire (a limited cross examination to test the qualifications of the witness) by opposing counsel and objections, the judge rules on whether the expert can continue to testify as an expert. Some courts do not allow the lawyer to use the word "expert" to refer to the expert witness. but the judge is still changed with the responsibility of determining if the witness is qualified as an expert. Yet no one uses the word "expert" in front of lay fact finders. The apparent reason for such a practice is, as explained below.

The 2000 Advisory Committee Notes to the amendment to Federal Rule of Evidence 702 says, in part:

"…The use of the term "expert" in the Rule does not, however, mean that a jury should actually be informed that a qualified witness is testifying as an "expert." Indeed, there is much to be said for a practice that prohibits the use of the term "expert" by both the parties and the court at trial. Such a practice "ensures that trial courts do not inadvertently put their stamp of authority" on a witness's opinion, and protects against the jury's being "overwhelmed by the so-called 'experts'."

More Tenders/Offers of the expert

"We believe that Mr. Taylor <u>should be permitted</u> to offer his opinions in this case."

"I <u>tender</u> Dr. Barron as an expert in the field of family medicine and request that she be allowed to testify as such.

"I <u>offer</u> Dr. Rosenberg as an expert in the field of neurology."

"Judge, we ask that the court <u>accept</u> Dr. Shigeta as an expert in civil engineering."

Offering the Opinion
Traditionally, the opinion is delivered in a two-question sequence:
Q1: Do you have an opinion as ….?
A: Yes
Q2: What is that opinion?

"Do you have an opinion, <u>within a reasonable degree of scientific certainty</u>, as to the time of death of Ms. X?"

"Do you have an opinion, <u>to a reasonable degree of medical probability</u>, as to whether the motorcycle accident caused Mr. Fulbright's epilepsy?"

"Do you have an opinion, <u>to a reasonable degree of engineering certainty</u>, as to whether the XXX caused the bridge to fail?"

"Do you have an opinion whether Mr. X suffered a brain damage as a result of the fight?"

Standards for Stating an Expert's Opinion
There are no minimum standards under FRE 702 describing how "good" an expert's opinion must be to be stated in court. By case law, some courts and jurisdictions require that the standard must be stated to a
"reasonable degree of [medical] <u>certainty</u>," or a
"reasonable degree of [scientific] <u>probability.</u>"
Other jurisdictions simply allow an expert to state an opinion without any specific qualification.
"What did your examination reveal?"

The above standards of "certainty" and "probability" are vague and rather unhelpful standards to a lay jury or courts-martial member who might be able to understand percentages, but who are given no guidance to the certainty or probability. Do those standards mean 51%, 65%, 75%, 85%, 95%, etc.? "Preponderance of the evidence" does have an associated percentage (50%+), but terms such as "sufficient to support a finding," "clear and convincing," "beyond a reasonable doubt," as well as "certainty" and "probability" do not. Simply, use whatever standard your judge and jurisdiction require.

In an attempt to be persuasive, some lawyers ask the experts questions like:

> "How positive are you of your opinion?"
> "What is the degree of your certainty?"

Inadmissible Information Reasonably Relied Upon

Experts can base their opinions on hearsay and other inadmissible evidence. FRE 703 says in part:

> "If experts in the particular field would reasonably rely on those kinds of facts or data in forming an opinion on the subject, they need not be admissible for the opinion to be admitted."

You should have in your tool chest of questions this question. "Is that the type of information reasonably relied upon by experts in your field?"

Remember

Whoever has the Biggest, Most Qualified Expert Might Win

Because opposing parties usually present opposing experts who have reached opposing conclusions, the advocacy principle is for you to try to present a more qualified and more credible expert than your opponent's expert. If "your" expert's testimony and conclusions are believed on the issue in dispute, you are more likely to win your case.

Other Books
by John Barkai

Federal Rules of Evidence Handbook with Common Objections &
Evidentiary Foundations

Humor in Negotiations & ADR: Cartoon Caption Contest Winners from
the ABA Dispute Resolution Magazine

Humor in Trial Evidence: Cartoon Caption Contest Winners and
Challenges from My Evidence Class

Military Rules of Evidence Handbook with Common Objections & Evidentiary
Foundations

Negotiation and Mediation Communication Gambits for Breaking Impasses and
More: What Do I Say When I Want To ...

The Pocket Guide to Common Trial Objections & Evidentiary Foundations

The following evidence books in my
Handbooks with Common Objections & Evidentiary Foundations series
are available exclusively on Amazon for the following states:

Alabama	Indiana	Nebraska	Rhode Island
Alaska	Iowa	Nevada	South Carolina
Arizona	Kentucky	New Hampshire	South Dakota
Arkansas	Louisiana	New Jersey	Tennessee
California **	Maine **	New Mexico	Texas **
Colorado	Maryland	North Carolina	Utah
Connecticut	Massachusetts	North Dakota	Vermont
Delaware	Michigan **	Ohio	Virginia
Florida **	Minnesota	Oklahoma	Washington
Georgia	Mississippi	Oregon	West Virginia
Hawaii	Montana	Pennsylvania **	Wisconsin
Idaho			Wyoming
Illinois			

** Also published "Just the Rules" books for these states.

Massachusetts, Missouri, and New York do not have rules of evidence,
but Massachusetts and New York have published "Guides" to evidence

Handbooks for the following Pacific Island jurisdictions.
which are supported by the 9th Circuit Federal Courts,
are also available on Amazon

American Samoa	Marshall Islands
Chuuk	Northern Mariana Islands
Federated States of Micronesia	Palau
Guam	Pohnpei
Kosrae	Yap

Also, handbooks for the U.S. Virgin Islands, Puerto Rico,
Australia, Bangladesh, Canada, India, Malaysia, New Zealand, Papua New Guinea,
Singapore, and Samoa

The author has "self-published" all the above books.
They are available exclusively on Amazon.com and are "print-on-demand."

To find Barkai's evidence and cartoon books

1. Go to the Amazon website – www.Amazon.com

2. Enter into the search bar: - John Barkai

Dedication

To my wife Linda ,and my adult twin daughters Hope, and Leah,
who bring me so much joy
and enrich my life
and
to the hundreds of my former evidence and clinical students
who learned these rules of evidence with me
over the past 45 years
at the William S. Richardson School of Law
at the University of Hawaii.

U.S. Federal Rules of Evidence
List of and Links to the Rules

https://www.law.cornell.edu/rules/fre
https://tinyurl.com/FREwithnotes

ARTICLE VI. WITNESSES

ARTICLE VII. OPINIONS AND EXPERT TESTIMONY

ARTICLE VIII. HEARSAY

ARTICLE IX. AUTHENTICATION AND IDENTIFICATION

ARTICLE X. CONTENTS OF WRITINGS, RECORDINGS, AND PHOTOGRAPHS

ARTICLE XI. MISCELLANEOUS RULES

Trial Skills Training Videos
University of Windsor
Faculty of Law
Clinical Law Education Program

https://www.youtube.com/playlist?list=PLLq5zcOX85J4ooPxLXsAtcxlZ
7QxEhJD6
(or search for YouTube Trial Skills Training Videos Windsor)

Professor Gemma Smyth of the University of Windsor Clinical Law Education Program has created 19 excellent training videos, which are posted on YouTube (see link address above) where students demonstrate trial skills and introduce evidence.

As described on the YouTube site, "In these videos, students view a mock criminal trial from start to finish. The trial is divided up into smaller portions that allow the student to understand the various components of a fairly simple criminal hearing."

The videos demonstrate general trial skills, including direct and cross examination, impeachment, entering evidence, closing arguments, and the judge announcing his judgments and giving his reasons for the judgement.

The image below shows how the videos are listed on YouTube, but the image is probably too small to be seen clearly in this handbook.

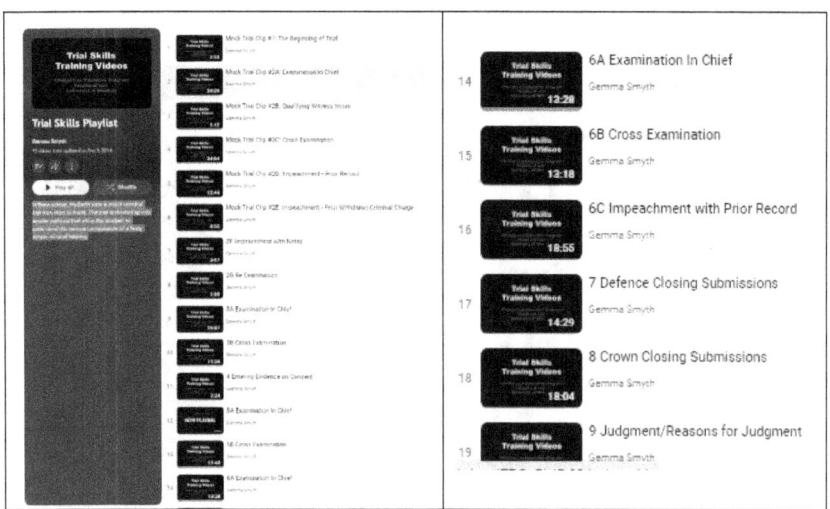

About the Author

Professor John Barkai is a former Detroit Michigan criminal trial lawyer, a fulltime law professor for 50 years - a Professor of Law at the William S. Richardson School of Law at the University of Hawaii for 45 years, and previously taught at Wayne State University in Detroit for 5 years. His major criminal trial practice experience was in 1972-1973 in Detroit, and included jury trials on charges for Murder, Criminal Sexual Conduct (then called Statutory Rape), Armed Robbery, Assault, and CCW (Carrying A Concealed Weapon). He has taught evidence since 1981 and has been the Director, and now Co-Director, of the Law School's Clinical Program since 1978. He has been a member of the Hawaii Supreme Court's Standing Committee on the Rules of Evidence since 1993. He has a B.B.A, M.B.A, and J.D, all from the University of Michigan. For the past 50 years, he has taught a criminal clinic in which his students try traffic and minor criminal cases under the state student practice rule. This handbook, and other similar handbooks, were inspired by handbooks he created in 2019 for a workshop for Pacific Island Judges from American Samoa, Marshall Islands, Federated States of Micronesia, Chuuk, Kosrae, Pohnpei, and Yap. He has published evidence handbooks similar to this one for all 50 states as well as 15 other jurisdictions from American Samoa to the U.S. Virgin Islands. He also has evidence and negotiation & ADR cartoon books on Amazon as well as a book on effective communication for negotiation and mediation.

www.ingramcontent.com/pod-product-compliance
Lightning Source LLC
Chambersburg PA
CBHW070332220526
45467CB00001B/122